PUBLIC
POLICY
MAKING

PUBLIC POLICY MAKING

Process and Principles

Larry N. Gerston

M.E. Sharpe
Armonk, New York
London, England

Library of Congress Cataloging-in-Publication Data

Gerston, Larry N.
Public policy making : process and principles / by
Larry N. Gerston.
p.   cm.
Includes bibliographical references and index.
ISBN 0-7656-0079-X (cloth alk. paper). — ISBN 0-7656-0080-3 (pbk. alk. paper).
1. Political planning—United States.   2. United States—Politics
and government.   3. Policy sciences.   I. Title.
JK468.P64G47   1997
320'.6'0973—dc21   96-29823
CIP
Printed in the United States of America

The paper used in this publication meets the minimum requirements of
American National Standard for Information Sciences—
Permanence of Paper for Printed Library Materials,
ANSI Z 39.48-1984.

BM (c)   10   9   8   7   6   5   4   3   2
BM (p)   10   9   8   7   6   5   4

For Elisa
The best policy maker in the business

CONTENTS

PREFACE

How does the political system *really* work, and why should we care? More than anything else, these two questions have provided much of the motivation for my teaching as well as the impetus for this book.

Too many times, institutional descriptions and flow charts of the political system bring about more confusion than clarity. They show diagrams and networks that are "official" but nevertheless fail to connect the polity's problems and possible outcomes. This occurs because the "system" is much more than a bunch of elected and appointed officials and their respective offices; rather it is a loosely structured (and sometimes seemingly convoluted) environment of conflicting conditions and complex solutions, almost all of which are in a constant state of flux.

Among the many sources of cynicism in the 1990s is the sense among casual observers that what we see is not consistent with formal descriptions of how things work. They wonder what keeps policy makers from doing some things and why political actors ostensibly removed from the policy making network manage to do others. That's where this book may help. It is designed to explain how the system works; as such, it is a tool for analysis, prediction, and perhaps participation.

Public Policy Making: Process and Principles places the element and dynamic circumstances of public policy in an analytical framework. Viewing the policy framework as a porous, changing entity, this book is designed to give you the political know-how for making sense out of the maze we call the *policy making process*. It takes us out of the world of orderly boxes and precise diagrams and into the universe of issues and policies that float in and out of the policy making arena.

In short, *Public Policy Making: Process and Principles* is intended as a "hands-on" description of what comes out of the political process. It's not particularly neat, but it is an approach to explaining how political life really works.

No single volume can fill in all the gaps about something as cavernous as the policy making process. Nevertheless, *Public Policy Making: Process and Principles* may serve as a starting point. Beyond everything else, I hope that the book clears up some of the mystery about how political decisions are made and carried out.

This book is the culmination of more than twenty years of learning and teaching about public policy. Even though it appears with my name, several of my colleagues at San Jose State University deserve credit for reading the manuscript and providing valuable suggestions. I am particularly grateful to Stephen Van Beek, who went through almost the entire manuscript and tendered invaluable advice. Ronald Sylvia and Peter Haas also took on sizable chunks of the manuscript, assuring that the final product would be much better than early drafts. At M. E. Sharpe, I extend my gratitude to Patricia Kolb, executive editor; Elizabeth Granda, program coordinator; and Ana Erlic, production editor.

Finally, a word of gratitude to the participants in my own policy making environment. My thanks go to my children Adam, Lee, and Rachel for putting up with so many "not now, maybe later" responses when I was mired in endless thought, and to Elisa, my wife, for enduring the way that I faded in and out of so many conversations as I struggled to make sense of my writing commitment.

PUBLIC
POLICY
MAKING

1 THE CONTEXT OF PUBLIC POLICY

In 1995, the 104th Congress began with Republican majorities in both houses for the first time in nearly fifty years. Promising less government wherever possible, the new leadership focused extensively on the nation's poverty "safety net" as an example of unnecessary "big government." Federal funds for school lunch programs, prenatal services, welfare programs, and dozens of other federally supported areas of assistance were substantially reduced, if not dismantled, as part of the Republican "Contract with America." Nevertheless, the $28 billion Food Stamp program was left intact, with only minor changes. Why? Could it be that the fervently conservative leadership had a hidden liberal streak after all? Not quite. Republican leaders simply realized that to eliminate this program would leave farmers without their subsidies, and since farmers were vital to the new coalition, that was one element of government assistance that the leadership could accept! This inconsistency points out the essence of the public policy making process.

The public policy making arena is fraught with confusion, contradictions, and consternation. Yet, whatever difficulties the student or practitioner may have in understanding the concept of policy making, it is a process that must be reckoned with.

Public policy is a relatively new subfield in political science. Its development as an area of study emerged out of the recognition that traditional analyses of government decisions were incomplete descriptions of political activities. As the relationships between society and its various public institutions have become more complex and more interdependent, the need has developed for more comprehensive assessments of what governments do, how they put their decisions into practice, and why they pursue some policy alternatives over others.

3

Focus on the public policy process has developed with the emergence of modern society and industrialization. Prior to the seventeenth and eighteenth centuries, most polities were consumed with self-survival and potential threats from foreign enemies. Political organization and infrastructure were largely irrelevant for obvious reasons: there were few decisions to make, and those who made them were dictators, monarchs, small bands of rulers, or unrepresentative legislative bodies. During the nineteenth century, representative government began to evolve in some parts of the world. With increased political participation by larger portions of the public, government decisions assumed greater importance and legitimacy. Clashing values with respect to social, economic, and political questions had profound implications for politics and government. With these changes, governments began to focus on the problems of their citizens.

These changes did not go unnoticed by those who studied political phenomena in the United States. As this young country matured, so did the approaches to the study of government and politics. Earlier in this century, American political scientists were content to analyze government in the context of its three major branches: the executive, the legislative, and the judicial.[1] While such studies were instructive about the powers of institutions, they were less than complete descriptions of the political process.

Fifty years later, political scientists expanded their perspectives of government activities. Some examinations centered on the informal relationship between interest groups and government, leading one scholar to conclude that political institutions "operate to order the relationships among various groups in society."[2] Other studies focused on the interdependence between government activities and diverse forces such as political parties or public opinion. Out of this evolution came the recognition of the symbiotic association between government and politics.[3]

Recent assessments in political science offer yet another slant on the powers and abilities of government bodies. Some contemporary scholars now argue that government is not designed to be merely responsive; nor, they assert, is government even neutral or benign. Instead, these writers contend that government institutions and officeholders possess powerful tools for altering social, economic, and technological arrangements. In light of the effects that policy makers have on society, we have come to appreciate that what comes *out* of government is as important as what goes in.[4] This thinking brings us to the concept of public policy. Viewed as a multifaceted approach to the study of politics, public policy making is a way of explaining the workings of modern government and the flow of political life.

In Search of a Framework

As an approach to understanding political change, public policy has almost as many definitions as there are policy issues. *Institutionalists*, those who concern themselves with the formal, observable building blocks of government, view public policy as a benign component of identified rules and procedures. As Lawrence Friedman writes, "in societies like ours . . . there arises an enormous demand—a need—for formal controls which have to come from some sort of organized government."[5] *Behavorialists*, scholars consumed with what people actually do, interpret public policy as the result of the interaction of powerful forces, some of which may be far removed from the halls of government. To that end, Calvin MacKenzie concludes, "law is a guide to public policy, a statement of policy makers hope policy will be; but it is not necessarily public policy."[6]

The debate over parameters is more than an exercise or game, for it is the word *process* that differentiates public policy from other approaches to government and politics. A process is dynamic and ongoing and, as such, is constantly subject to reevaluation, cessation, expedited, or even erratic movement. Conceptually speaking, then, policy making exists in an open environment with neither a beginning nor an end, and with virtually no boundaries. What seems inconceivable as a policy issue one day may well be the focal point of heated debate the next. Within this nomadic context, our task is to examine public policy making as a concept, as a process, and as a mechanism of political change.

While there is little concurrence among scholars on the framework of the public policy making arena, they tend to agree on a core of basic assumptions. Most obviously, *government activities and commitments are crucial to the meaning of public policy*. Defense, welfare, transportation, education, and agriculture are but a few major areas of historical concern to government. Other areas of interest, such as space exploration, the environment, and biotechnology, are relatively new government concerns. However, the history of government fascination with a policy area is not as important as the attention itself. Without government involvement and direction, there is no public policy.

Another point upon which analysts agree is that *sizable portions of society and its resources are affected by public policies.* Whether we speak of consumers, the disabled, automobile drivers, handgun owners, or acquired immune deficiency syndrome (AIDS) victims, each of these constituencies and countless others are likely to be affected by many public policies. Some policies, such as defense, taxation, or public education, affect almost everyone. In fact, most people's lives are directly influenced by many public policies simultaneously. However, only a few public policy commitments consciously concern people at any one time.

Finally, virtually all students and practitioners of public policy concur that *policy making is a process.* The search for, debate about, development of, application of, and evaluation of a given policy spring from a continuum of events, with a beginning that is almost impossible to pinpoint and an end that is rarely permanent. Whatever the issue in question, scholars agree that public policy making has a perpetual, dynamic, and evolutionary quality.

A Working Definition of Public Policy

Aside from these basic areas of consensus, policy analysts differ greatly on the basis and limits of the public policy field. Consider the following definitions from three leading political scientists: Thomas Dye characterizes public policy as the study of "what governments do, why they do it, and what difference it makes."[7] Seeking to extend linkage, B. Guy Peters adds that public policy is the "sum of government activities, whether acting directly or through agents, as it has an influence on the lives of citizens."[8] Conversely, David Robertson and Dennis Judd take a more restrained course by casting government as the independent variable—that is, the crucial intersection of change—not only in terms of crafting current policies but with respect to future demands for different policies.[9]

These approaches and others all have merit and individually address key components of the policy making process. However, for our purposes, we seek a definition that responds to the actions and exchanges of both people and governments in a dynamic, interdependent manner. Thus, *public policy* is defined here as *the combination of basic deci-*

sions, commitments, and actions made by those who hold or affect government positions of authority. In most instances, these arrangements result from interactions among those who demand change, those who make decisions, and those who are affected by the policy in question. The determinations made by those in positions of legitimate authority—most commonly, one or more public offices in government—are subject to possible redirection in response to pressures from those outside government as well as from others within government.

The linkage between policy makers and policy receivers is vital to understanding the meaning and power of public policy. In a very direct sense, society benefits or suffers because of government activity. Sometimes, both experiences may occur simultaneously. At a minimum, the more controversial a proposed policy or policy area, the more likely it is that one part of society may benefit at the expense of another segment. Furthermore, the variety of potential public policy questions is so great that some government decisions emerging from the political process have greater impacts on society than others. The simple fact is that each public policy question has its own unique impact on those who lie in its path.

Public policies result from the blend of politics and government. David Easton defines politics as "the authoritative allocation of values."[10] Public policy, then, is as important in defining prevailing values (politics) as it is in defining solutions to prevailing problems (through government). In a very real sense, values predetermine public policies, although the values of some parts of society will often be more influential on a policy than the values of others.

Components of the Public Policy Process

The methods of public policy analysis differ from those used in the "hard" sciences. Social science revolves around needs, emotions, unanticipated events, and a good deal of irrationality. These characteristics are extremely difficult to quantify or duplicate, and they rarely produce consensus regarding any order of importance or rank. Such is not the case in other disciplines.

Although the formulas themselves may be complicated or esoteric, the laws of physics, mathematics, and other sciences have a predictability that captures a certain respect from social scientists. In these fields, the hypothetical problem of 2 + 2 will *always* yield 4 regardless of inflation, war, unemployment, disease, or any number of factors that may affect society. Such accuracy does not occur in the study of public policy. However, some components are constant in the public policy universe. They are:

- Issues that appear on the public agenda
- Actors who present, interpret, and respond to those issues
- Resources affected by those issues
- Institutions that deal with issues
- The levels of government that address issues.

Perhaps the most critical of these components is the determination of which policy issues will be resolved in the public sector, although the ability to respond to them may often be defined by the desire to do something and the resources available. In addition to describing public policy areas and their costs, it is necessary to identify the actors and the formal structures of government that may be the drivers of resolution. Finally, it is important to determine which levels of government are best equipped to make policy. Public policy may be developed *horizontally*, with several agencies coordinating efforts at the national, the state, or the local level. Policy may also be developed *vertically*; in this approach, the decisions made at one level—commonly the national—are carried out on behalf of all parties or perhaps assigned to another level—often the states—for execution. As we will see below, these five ingredients highlight the complexities of making public policy.

Policy Issues

We can compare commonly discussed areas of public policy to a revolving ferris wheel at an amusement park. The wheel operates with a consistent pattern; it travels for a fixed period of time, stops, then proceeds again. While the wheel's movement is predictable, the entries, departures, and combinations of the passengers are not. Sometimes the wheel is almost full, but at other times it is nearly empty. A few passengers may opt to ride the wheel for several turns, while a single cycle will suffice for others. Public policy issues are the "passengers" that move off and on the "wheels" of government. Some, such as the debate over abortion, have incredible staying power; others, such as the discussion over reducing federal gasoline taxes in 1996, disappear quickly after their emergence.

Although policy areas include a range of ever-changing public needs, the types of issues can be divided into two broad categories: *substantive* and *symbolic*. Substantive issues are those areas of controversy that have a major impact on society. Regulation of the economy, welfare reform, civil rights legislation, and environmental protection are examples of substantive public policy issues. Because of their comprehensive impact, substantive issues are usually quite difficult to resolve and may linger on the public agenda for long periods of time.

Symbolic issues center on irritating public problems and "quick fixes" to get them off the public agenda. Responses to these issue areas tend to provide more psychological relief than actual change in the political system. Outcomes are generally uncontroversial because the policy commitment does not threaten major shifts of social, economic, or political capital. For example, legislation by Congress in 1995 that removed members' exemption from employment regulations affecting the rest of society assuaged public anger rather than effecting any significant change.

Sometimes, substantive issues are addressed by symbolic responses, generating a good deal of resentment as a consequence. For example, in 1994 many congressional candidates rode the illegal immigration issue to victory. The suddenly explosive issue led the Clinton administration to respond by increasing the number of U.S. border patrol guards, leading many critics to cry "tokenism," or a symbolic response to a substantive issue. The issue lingered longer than many had expected, and in 1996 there was a more substantive response, with provisions in the Welfare Reform Act that denied welfare benefits to illegal and legal immigrants. Both substantive and symbolic policy agendas are discussed in chapter 3.

Actors

How do policy issues get their "tickets" to the public policy "ride"? Unlike matters that remain solely private or as individual problems, public policy issues gain their status when they reach the eyes and ears of government actors. As we will see in chapter 2, *triggering mechanisms* transport once-private matters into the public forum of discussion. From this point on, policy makers may seize various public issues and try to formulate appropriate responses.

Issues are generated from a variety of sources. Sometimes problems are presented by individuals who are outside government altogether;

for example, a celebrity who falls victim to a terrible disease or accident may, because of his or her notoriety, raise public consciousness. At other times, an investigation or exposé by a prominent media representative may serve as the conduit to government leaders. Then again, the people who are in government and closest to the policy making process may advance an issue and generate support for resolution.

Resources

Recognizing problems is one part of the policy making process; deciding how to pay the price to solve them is another. Sometimes, policy makers have targeted those responsible for a problem to pay for it. For example, when Congress passed the 1990 Clean Air Act, the legislation committed the United States to a massive antipollution program— but at a significant cost to polluters. Compliance with the law's new standards forced producers and users of pollution-controlling materials to pick up much of the tab. Thus, within three years, the sticker price of a new automobile had increased by $225, gasoline had edged up between 3 and 5 cents per gallon, and even the costs of products ranging from dry-cleaning services to refrigerators went up to meet the requirements of the new law.[11] On other occasions, public policy makers have elected to use national revenues as the source of payment for a program. Nowhere is this more evident than in our foreign policy commitments. Thus, when presidents have committed troops and weapons to such places as Iraq or Bosnia, the tab has been picked up by the taxpayers. Most of the time, the public is deferential on such issues. Nevertheless, the fact that such commitments are sometimes made without a thorough national airing may backfire on leaders, as was the case when President Lyndon Johnson's pursuit of the Vietnam War during the mid-1960s ultimately cost him his office.[12]

What makes policy makers commit resources for some policies and not for others? Values, the extent of a crisis, awareness, and other factors enter into the equation that determines the answer. But the availability of resources plays a large part as well.

Public Institutions

Public institutions are the vehicles through which public policies are formulated and carried out. The word *institution* rings of formality and organization, but it also suggests the routes for traffic traveling through the policy process. Aside from occasional policies mandated by the electorate at the state and local levels, the basic policy making institutions are the executive, legislative, and judicial branches of government. Bureaucracies and regulatory agencies are also prominent in the creation and implementation of public policies.

The Executive Branch

Numerous examples highlight the roles of institutions and their strategists in the development of public policy. More often than not, the "checks and balances" organization of government requires the various branches to act in complementary fashion. However, there are occasions when a single element of government can frame, if not dominate, the policy process. When presidents, for example, sign executive orders to limit discrimination or prevent strike breakers from assuming permanent positions in the federal workplace, they wield their power to make policy. Likewise, when presidents send weapons or U.S. troops to other countries in crisis situations, they direct public policy in the arena of foreign affairs. A very large portion of any president's leadership stems from his ability to establish priorities and define policy commitments.

The Legislative Branch

As the nation's chief legislative body, Congress makes policy with the hundreds of statutes or laws it enacts each year. The ability to make these decisions gives Congress a major role in guiding the nation. The Republican "Contract with America," a campaign tool for more than 300 House of Representatives candidates and incumbents in 1994, became the framework for a good deal of domestic policy making effort by the new Republican majority in 1995. Much of the program was either tempered in the Senate or vetoed by President Bill Clinton and, in fact, became a useful foil for Clinton's reelection in 1996. Nevertheless, this legislative agenda demonstrated the power of Congress to assert itself in the policy making arena, and many Republican observers believed that despite the demise of the Contract with America, key elements such as its call for a balanced budget and welfare reform were adopted anyway by President Clinton.[13]

The Judiciary

Although courts are not active in the legislative process, they also play an important role in policy making. Courts establish policy through interpretation of the law, sometimes to the chagrin of Congress. One such example occurred over the "freedom of expression" issue. In 1989, the U.S. Supreme Court struck down a Texas law that made it illegal for an individual to desecrate an American flag. Outraged, the Congress passed the federal Flag Protection Act in 1989, only to see it struck down by the Court in 1990 as an infringement against First Amendment guarantees.[14] Some members of Congress then introduced a constitutional amendment on the issue, but they failed to gain the required two-thirds approval in either house.

The Bureaucracy

The three branches mentioned above are recognized staples of American government. Yet, the policy making process includes a number of other, less obvious governmental actors. The bureaucracy, a collection of agencies designed to carry out relatively specific tasks, has become so vital in modern society that it is commonly described as the "fourth branch" of government. Officially, most bureaucratic agencies administer policies created by Congress and the White House. Yet, it is often difficult to determine where the administration of policy ends and policy making begins. Even the lowest-level bureaucrat may have the power to make decisions and, hence, to establish policy.

Regulatory Agencies

Regulatory agencies constitute yet another element in the policy making process. For the better part of the twentieth century, the Interstate Commerce Commission (ICC), the Federal Trade Commission (FTC), and dozens of other boards and commissions have been active partners in making the decisions of government. These bodies have been created in waves, first to deal with economic issues such as trade and commerce, and more recently to focus on social problems.[15] Although a consensus seems to exist regarding the value of most economic regulatory units, considerable disagreement has emerged in recent years over the wisdom of regulatory bodies dealing with social issues such as environmental protection and employment discrimination.[16]

We have noted how policy making institutions and their authorities execute several valuable functions. They organize issues for the public agenda and, under the right circumstances, convert them into public commitments. But once a policy has been created, its success or failure depends upon the extent to which it is carried out. This is *implementation,* an activity that turns official policy commitments into reality. Many of the policy actors cited above share responsibility for this function, as discussed more fully in chapter 5.

Federalism—The Sharing of Power among Governments

The fifth component of the public policy making process centers on the participant levels of government. Just as the roles of government have grown throughout the twentieth century, the numbers of governments responding to issues have also increased. More than ever, governments are sharing policy making functions and responsibilities. This evolution suggests major changes in *federalism,* defined here as the political and legal framework within which different levels of governments interact.

The extent to which intergovernmental relations have changed is the subject of some debate. Using the 1930s as a watershed mark, Michael Reagan and John Sanzone find substantial differences in the ways governments make policies. The chief change has been in the shift of policy making responsibility primarily to the national level: "If we compare the reach of the federal government today with that which existed prior to World War II, . . . the range of public sector decisions subject to national government influence is immeasurably greater now."[17] Others are not so convinced that such sweeping changes remain in place. Thus, Virginia Gray and her colleagues conclude, the national government "has grown increasingly reluctant to undertake new domestic policy initiatives, especially expensive ones."[18] While these two conclusions do not show federalism in the same light, their authors acknowledge the struggle for and distribution of power at multiple levels of government.

Until now, we have focused on the levels of *formal* governments that take part in the public policy process. Yet, some *citizens* may also initiate policy from outside traditional government structures. About half of the state governments—mostly in the West—and virtually all local governments have referendums and/or initiatives as policy making tools. In most cases, a referendum allows voters to decide on policies drafted by a legislature or a local government body, whereas an initiative permits voters to propose modifications in the constitution, charter laws, or ordinances, which are then accepted or rejected at the next election.[19] Many initiative and referendum questions cover extremely complex questions. Nevertheless, in recent years voters in various states have decided on policy questions on topics such as euthanasia, legalized gambling, immigration, and capital punishment. This method of participation not only brings citizens directly into the public policy making process, but also awakens national leaders to emergent issues.

Sometimes, state or national public officials make policy decisions that conflict with another level of government. When such clashes occur, they are usually settled by the federal courts. Thus, in 1994 when California enacted an initiative that denied government social services to illegal immigrants, much of the new law was overturned by a U.S. District Court because of the law's interference with the Equal Protection clause found in the Fourteenth Amendment to the U.S. Constitution. Conversely, when Congress enacted a law in 1990 that established "gun-free" school zones, the U.S. Supreme Court overturned the legislation because of Congress' assumption of local police powers. Such are the uncertainties of the policy making process because of federalism.

Federalism has emerged as a crucial policy making element. Although the pressure points of the political process extend in both vertical directions (among levels) and horizontal directions (among branches) of government, most of the discussion in the following chapters will focus on the national government's responses to policy issues. It is at this level that questions with the widest application are presented, debated, and resolved.

Contemporary Trends in Public Policy

Between the late 1930s and the 1980s, American government expanded its role in society. During this period, the proportion of public expenditures to the nation's income increased dramatically. One study of federal activity shows that, between 1951 and 1976, the national government's budget outlays alone grew from 14.7 percent to 22.8 percent of the gross domestic product (GDP).[20] Federal commitments reached 24 percent of the GDP in 1990, but recent statistics suggest a

Figure 1.1 **Federal Budget Outlays, 1950–95** (as a percent of GDP)

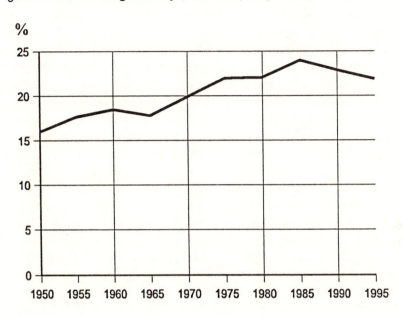

Source: U.S. Office of Management and Budget, *Historical Tables*, annuals (Washington, DC, 1996).

possible long-term retrenchment, or at least a slowdown of the government's public spending. In 1991, federal spending as a percentage of the GDP began to decrease to about the 20 percent level, marking a reversal in the role of government. The expenditure percentages have hovered at this level for the past several years.[21] (See Figure 1.1.)

Why the redirection? Some speculate that the end of the Cold War and massive defense spending are responsible for the new direction. Others note the generally negative perception of unnecessary, if not bloated, federal government, many commitments from which go to questionable domestic spending areas of activity. In fact, both contentions have assumed high visibility on the public agenda, and changes have occurred as a result of this attention.

In the area of defense, annual federal governments dropped precipitously from $328 billion in 1990 to a projected $250 billion in 1997, a slide of 24 percent in seven years. As a result, military personnel and defense procurements have been reduced dramatically.[22]

Cuts in the domestic arena have followed, as critics have become increasingly vocal about a national government out of control. In 1993 President Clinton appointed the Bipartisan Commission on Entitlement and Tax Reform, to determine the legitimacy of such claims and put forth recommendations for change. One year later, the commission concluded that, by 2012, entitlement benefits such as Social Security, Medicare, Medicaid, and federal civil service pensions together would consume nearly all government revenues, leaving no money for defense, environment, highways, or any other area of need.[23] Equally significant, when the twenty-two-member commission turned to recommendations, the participants could not agree on what to do!

Much of the current debate over policy objectives centers on the questionability of the national government to meet society's needs at a time when resources are no longer as endless as they once seemed. Conventional wisdom once suggested that American ingenuity and technology would enhance our lives on a regular basis. Indeed, the mere possibility of *slowed* growth has been heretical to a society where, for most, fulfillment of the "American dream" has been a routine expectation and accomplishment. Increasingly, futurists fear a future with a series of built-in scarcities and broken dreams. Lester Thurow, for one, rattles off a list of social and economic problems that have escalated in size and seriousness, and that are spiked by the ability of government to solve them.[24] Others, such as David Osborne and Ted Gaebler, view the crisis as an opportunity for governments to "reinvent" themselves, with market-driven programs and decentralized management.[25] Either way, the possible allocation of fewer public benefits for society only underscores the importance of understanding the public policy process.

As the nation prepares to leave one century and to enter the next, the most controversial elements of American public policy seem to be in three broad areas: *social issues, economic issues,* and *technological issues.* Each of these has a decidedly domestic tone, although none is completely without influence from foreign factors. All these issues share a common bond: They draw attention to defining the "proper" extent of government commitments. In this regard, they reflect the contemporary concerns of American politics.

Social Issues

While social issues are hardly new to the American political mosaic, government response to them is largely a recent phenomenon. For most of this country's two centuries, governments tended to minimize their roles in any activities that involved social change or assistance. Even in such areas as welfare relief and care for the elderly, compelling questions by today's standards, and public policies were conspicuously absent. The lack of government attention was not based on economics so much as on a conservative political tradition steeped in the virtues of individualism.

Attitudes toward welfare and other social questions underwent reassessment during the Great Depression of the 1930s. Until that time, a few states and local governments dealt with relief on a minimal basis. But after President Franklin Roosevelt urged, and the Congress passed, the Social Security Act of 1935, governments became immersed in social issues that had previously been viewed as private matters. Aid to the poor, medical research, and health care are but a few of the social issue offshoots that have received government attention as a result of the seeds sown during Roosevelt's "New Deal." Further attention was generated during the 1960s, when U.S. social policies included urban renewal, abortion funding, and federal aid for education, largely inspired by President Lyndon Johnson's "Great Society."

Despite the debate over government involvement in social issues, some responses have garnered more consensus than others. Social Security, for example, has generally been taken off the agenda as a controversial issue. Medicaid, a program providing medical assistance for the elderly indigent population, has been susceptible to some debate. And federally funded abortions have become so controversial that Congress has eliminated financial support in most instances. Still other issues, such as capital punishment or federal funding for private schools, have found so little agreement that the national government has steered away from any significant policy commitments.

Economic Issues

Governments respond to economic problems because of the widely held sentiment that society should operate with some sense of security. However, whether the benefits accrue in the form of wage guarantees, subsidies, or safety, the costs for providing such protection are ultimately passed on to the public. Debates over the necessity of a given economic policy, weighing both costs and benefits, may be divisive.

Nevertheless, government leaders have as their responsibility the task of developing policies and services to match public needs.

Economic policies tend to be controversial because they have uneven impacts on society's members. The most serious economic issue areas involve two major themes: the appropriate extent of government involvement in the economy and income redistribution through taxation. Both areas have received a "walking-on-eggshells" treatment in American politics. As the economy has become more complex and more interdependent, some critics have called for government to referee the disputes between private business interests; others have been equally adamant in demanding that the private and public sectors be kept as far apart as possible. Income redistribution issues have been controversial because of the tension between the "haves" and the "have-nots," and because of the debate over what, if anything, government should do to alter such disparities through progressive taxation.

Several government bodies create economic policies for Americans. They are particularly powerful at the national level, where economic policies not only affect the most people but also influence lower government structures. The Federal Reserve Board and the president's Council of Economic Advisors are just two of several agencies concerned with economic issues. The Federal Reserve Board has substantial control over credit, interest rates, and other important facets of the economy. The Council of Economic Advisors guides the president on long-term economic problems like inflation, recessions, employment cycles, and balance-of-payments difficulties. Although these institutions contribute much to the resolution of thorny economic questions, their work is not widely followed or understood.

Economic public policy issues are predicated to a large extent upon the political values held by individuals, society, and government. Moreover, often the resolution of an economic issue is tied closely to the resolution of a social issue. If, for example, the national government commits to a balanced budget, reduced expenditures for low-income families might foster social disruption. Conversely, if the national government commits to a spending format that ignores the balanced budget imperative, repeated deficits may cause inflation, leaving unhappy citizens with less purchasing power. Thus, the management of economic questions can have broad implications for all sectors of American society.

Technological Issues

From a philosophical perspective, technology has always represented a challenge to society. Ever since the Industrial Revolution, scholars have written about the drawbacks and improvements that technology seems to provide for the political order.[26] In their research on comparative politics, Gabriel Almond and G. Bingham Powell note the direct impact of technological growth on urbanization, education, communication, and countless other forms of political, economic, and social activity. Several consequences of technological change—notably, weak family structures, psychological alienation, and uncertain economic conditions—present formidable problems for the political system.[27] Given our long history of technological evolution, American society is particularly susceptible to these difficulties.

With the emergence of the postindustrial age, the tendency has been to let technology take its own course, independently of government oversight. Yet, developments have moved faster than society's ability to cope with them. With respect to life issues, artificial respirators and other mechanical life-support systems have led to new problems in defining life and death. Automation has eliminated millions of low-tech jobs, while creating millions of high-tech opportunities. The global reliance upon fossil fuels has increased global prosperity as well as "global warming," a condition that threatens to choke the earth in its own, normally beneficial natural atmosphere. The ironies are almost daunting.

It now appears that reliance on technology cannot continue without adequate safeguards for society. As technologist Rudi Volti notes, the proliferation of knowledge has produced a dizzying pace of change. "But for technology to be truly beneficial, . . . [o]ur challenge will be to develop and apply many different kinds of knowledge—ethical, philosophical, sociological, political and economic, so that we can do a better job of defining our real needs and creating the technologies that serve them."[28] To this, Theodore Lowi responds, "The increased pace of technological change in our epoch seems only to make the need for administration more intense" in the name of sound, well-thought-out public policies.[29]

In summary, public policy authorities deal with many social, economic, and technological issues. The public agenda—the list of questions awaiting governmental disposition—is carved from these areas of concern. Given the multitude of issues and the large number of policy making agencies, the agenda is perpetually full and ripe for action.

A Look Ahead

The creation of public policy is a dynamic process. Events, actors, and political institutions combine and conflict in a wide array of unpredictable ways. Yet, there is a general method through which basic questions are raised, considered, and perhaps decided. The rest of this book addresses that process as well as those junctures where the process may break down. The following chapters address the elements of policy making process as well as specific issue areas.

Chapter 2, the first of a series of linked chapters, describes triggering mechanisms and how they generate public policy issues. Chapter 3 discusses the problems of agenda building. In chapter 4, major policy actors are defined and cataloged. Chapter 5 traces the policy process to the point of implementation and considers the factors that impede or encourage actual application of public policies emerging from the political arena. Chapter 6 covers evaluation, the means for assessing the extent to which public policies have been carried out vis-à-vis their original design. In chapter 7, we review the basic elements of the policy making process as they relate to the larger contexts of values and politics.

The concepts and tools provided in this book should help with the analysis of virtually any policy issue, whether national or local in significance. Why? Because policy making is a process filled with never-ending issues, competing approaches to their solutions, and conflict over their implementation.

Questions for Further Thought

1. It has been written that public policy making is process-driven. Explain the significance of this concept.

2. Discuss the stages of the public policy making process. How do these components frame what goes into or out of the policy making machinery?

3. The stakes in the policy making process are higher today than in the past. What accounts for this change?

Suggested Reading

Abraham, Henry J., *The Judiciary: The Supreme Court in the Governmental Process*, 9th ed. (Dubuque, IA: Brown and Benchmark, 1991).

Anderson, James E., *Public Policymaking*, 2d ed. (Boston: Houghton Mifflin, 1994).

Cochran, Clarke, Lawrence C. Mayer, T.R. Carr, and N. Joseph Cayer, *American Public Policy*, 4th ed. (New York: St. Martin's Press, 1993).

Dolbeare, Kenneth M., *American Public Policy* (New York: McGraw-Hill, 1982).

Dye, Thomas R., *American Federalism* (Lexington, MA: Lexington, 1990).

Mezey, Michael, *Congress, the President, and Public Policy* (Boulder, CO: Westview, 1989).

Naisbitt, John, *Megatrends* (New York: Warner, 1982).

Ripley, Randall B., and Grace A. Franklin, *Congress, the Bureaucracy and Public Policy*, 5th ed. (Pacific Grove, CA: Brooks/Cole, 1991).

Rushefsky, Mark E., *Public Policy in the United States* (Pacific Grove, CA: Brooks/Cole, 1990).

Stone, Deborah A, *Policy Paradox and Political Reason* (Glenview, IL: Scott/Foresman, 1988).

Tolchin, Susan J., and Martin Tolchin, *Dismantling America* (New York: Oxford University Press, 1985).

2 TRIGGERING MECHANISMS: CATALYSTS FOR PUBLIC POLICIES

Public policies spring from issues that trouble a segment or segments of society to the point of taking action. Issues preceding those policies develop when individuals with similar problems are forced to cope, without solution, for an unacceptable period of time. The word *problem* could be an invitation to semantic confusion. Commonly speaking, everyone has problems in the course of daily life. Getting through the hectic workday, coping with miserable traffic congestion, and even cramming for too many exams at the same time are problems with which we are all too familiar. However, the difficulties that sow the seeds of public policy decisions fall into a unique category. The individuals or groups who suffer these circumstances rely on government action to change their unfavorable condition into an acceptable situation.

Of course, one person's problem could be another's pleasure. That a domestic autoworker is laid off due to a slumping demand for American cars may be a positive development for a salesperson who works at an import dealership. Under such circumstances, agreement on the definition of the problem (i.e., the perception of poorly built, expensive American cars versus unfair foreign competition because of inexpensive labor) may not occur, thus leaving potential policy questions unformulated and certainly unresolved. The lack of consensus leaves individuals unable to establish a common framework of public issues. As Robert Eyestone explains, in the stages prior to government action, "there is no official agency for sanctioning a single definition of a social problem."[1] Given the absence of widespread public consensus, there is little likelihood of securing interest in the policy making arena.

A public problem requiring government response seems to be something that is more pervasive than a personal difficulty, and the concern of large numbers of individuals with the same problem may transform that question into a public policy issue. Nevertheless, all problems begin as individual issues, and it is the evolution of personal topics into widely shared aggravation that makes such dilemmas suddenly political and, therefore, candidates for public policy activity. What phenomenon promotes this transfer? What is it that changes an everyday difficulty into a public debate? The answer is a concept known as the *triggering mechanism.*

In the context of the political process, a *triggering mechanism* is *a critical event (or set of events) that converts a routine problem into a widely shared, negative public response.* This public response, in turn, is the basis for the policy issue that ensues in the wake of the triggering event. When an occurrence crystallizes a negative condition into a pressing political demand for change, the metamorphosis happens because of the staying power of the triggering mechanism.

Triggering mechanisms are important in reordering the consciousness levels of both the public and the public policy makers. However, their predictability is another matter altogether. John Kingdon describes the conditions for triggering mechanisms as "policy windows" that open and shut in unexpected intervals: "Once the window opens, it does not stay open for long. An idea's time comes, but it also passes. . . . [And] if the window passes without action, it may not open again for a long time."[2]

Inasmuch as society's priorities change with social, economic, and political conditions, events that might generate strong reactions at one point in history may have a negligible impact on another point in time. Consider our changing attitudes toward poverty. Until the 1930s, dominant U.S. public opinion embraced the idea that the poor, relatively small in numbers, were responsible for their own destiny. Yet, the Great Depression of 1929 soon changed many perceptions about poverty. Between 1929 and 1931, the number of unemployed workers jumped from three million to eight million. By 1933, the ranks of the unemployed swelled to fifteen million, or approximately one-third of the entire labor force, and countless Americans previously unaffected by poverty suddenly experienced the condition on a personal basis. Viewed in a public policy context, the Great Depression served as the triggering mechanism for Franklin Roosevelt's presidential election in 1932 and for the subsequent flood of New Deal legislation.

Not all triggering mechanisms are as obvious as, or have the impact of, the Great Depression of 1929. In fact, the effects of a triggering mechanism vary considerably. For example, public opinion surveys during the early 1990s repeatedly showed concern about out-of-control health costs and overwhelming demand for health care reform; yet, after months of hearings and debates, President Clinton and Congress failed to agree on any changes in the status quo.[3] During the same period, when Congress proposed to solve persistent annual national government deficits with a balanced budget amendment, a vocal minority protested that such an enactment would undermine the nation's Social Security system. As a result, the amendment failed by a single vote and brought disappointment, if not anger, from political conservatives.

Aside from obvious disruptions such as economic depression, military aggression, and natural disaster, the effects of most triggering mechanisms on the public policy process are ascertained post hoc by observing reactions to an event itself. If a development or an action attracts considerable public attention and widespread demand for change, then it is considered to be a triggering mechanism. If the development goes by without sizable reaction, then it is not.

Triggering mechanisms develop in internal (domestic) and external (foreign) environments. Most of the time, we concern ourselves with internal triggering mechanisms because our policy focus and our resource commitments have a decidedly domestic orientation, particularly since the end of the Cold War. Sometimes, matters become particularly complicated because of the impact of an external triggering mechanism on internal public policy decisions.

Triggering Mechanism Factors

Triggering mechanisms perform a vital function at an early juncture in the public policy making process: they identify and clarify emerging issues. Unfortunately, these activities are difficult to anticipate because they tend to remain "hidden" from view, as their momentum builds behind more observable daily events. Nevertheless, triggering mechanisms become important to the political process when their ramifications present adverse effects for a large sector of the public under a specific set of conditions at a particular point in time. Their interference with routine tells the impacted segment of society that something is "wrong" and in need of attention.

Unexpected as they are, triggering mechanisms are important because of their potential for altering the boundaries of the political system. What is not necessarily part of the political process prior to a triggering mechanism may become the subject of political decisions after a triggering event has taken place. Thomas Dye writes that public policy activities "are heavily influenced by the nature of the environment."[4] As events from the environment penetrate the boundaries of the political system, they rearrange that system. Thus, although their significance is often unforeseen or underestimated at the time of their occurrence, triggering mechanisms help define new problems and subsequent policy response options.

The value of a triggering mechanism as a catalyst for public policy stems from the interaction of three factors: *scope*, *intensity*, and *time*. Together, these factors constitute the core ingredients of the demands for political change. The presence of each factor in combination with the others establishes the potential impact of the triggering mechanism on the public policy process, as well as the likelihood for change. The sections below elaborate on the various aspects of triggering mechanisms and their relationships to the public policy process.

Scope

Scope refers to the number of people affected by the triggering mechanism. If an event has widespread implications for a sizable sector of society, then the demand for action will have a broad base. However, if the triggering mechanism has altered the lives of relatively few people, then it may be difficult for them to "make their case" and, hence, gain acknowledgment from political actors who have the capability to effect change.

Physical parameters and policy jurisdictions interact with scope. If, for example, a toxic spill occurs in a large city, the scope of the issue may be considerable for that area, yet rather insignificant elsewhere. Local leaders may be catapulted into action, while national public policy makers may remain unaware of or disinterested in the problem. However, if similar toxic spills take place in other areas or toxicity is found throughout the nation's water systems, then the scope of the events will change as well. Similarly, when a hurricane pounds a populous area like the Gulf Coast or the Eastern seaboard, the scope of its damage is far greater than if the storm wreaked havoc on Puerto Rico.

Does this mean that isolated disasters are less important than widespread disasters? Certainly not in terms of those people who are affected. Nevertheless, the sheer numbers affected by a disaster may determine much about the stakes. For this reason, the dramatic nature of triggering mechanisms lies in the narrowness or breadth of the potential public segment affected by unanticipated events.

Intensity

A second factor in determining the impact of triggering mechanisms is the intensity of the event perceived by the public. If an unanticipated incident receives a mild reception, then the subsequent attitudes toward the event will not dictate the need for any policy change. However, if the event captures concern, particularly in the form of fear or anger, then public policy makers are likely to pay attention to the clamor before them. One such example occurred with the discovery of raw sewage, medical waste, and other dangerous debris up and down the East Coast in 1988, as a result of antiquated sewage systems and the dumping of waste 100 miles offshore. Residents roared in anger and demanded protection as local government leaders blamed each other. With the fear of similar disasters spreading to virtually all coastal areas, Congress responded almost instantaneously with the Ocean Dumping Act of 1988.[5]

In contrast to offshore pollution reaction is the public's response to the relationship between tobacco and cancer. For more than a third of this century, medical researchers in and out of government have demonstrated a "cause-and-effect" linkage between the two elements. Yet, the responses have been limited to slight declines in per capita consumption patterns and minor limitations on advertising; the demands for government constraints on tobacco use have been mild and limited. Given little public interest and pressure, the issue has received minimal attention from public policy makers, except to the extent that such materials provide user taxes. Even when President Clinton demanded the regulation of tobacco during the 1996 campaign, the topic quickly went up in smoke as a campaign issue.

Time

The length of time during which a critical event unfolds is the third factor fundamental to the determination of a triggering mechanism as a catalyst for policy activity. Whereas some events seem to transpire almost immediately, others go through a lengthy gestation process. There is no necessary correlation between the length of a triggerring mechanism's development and the potence of the event; that which transpires instantly can be just as powerful as something that comes to pass over a germination cycle.

One virtually instantaneous triggering mechanism occurred with the release of nuclear waste into river water and the subsequent nuclear plant shutdown at Three Mile Island, Pennsylvania, in 1979. Within days of the incident, the public and the public policy makers alike began to engage in widespread discussions of the risks of nuclear power and the potential for radiation disaster at the more than 100 nuclear power plant facilities across the United States.

Other events require long lead times before the public becomes sufficiently aroused to demand change. One such instance has been the basis for public dialogue about human immunodeficiency virus (HIV) and the deadly disease AIDS. When this disease was first discovered during the early 1980s, most people remained either unaware of it or unconcerned with its lethal nature. Even most people who were famil-iar with AIDS were minimally interested because of the disease's reputation as a plague associated with homosexuals or drug users, but as more and more individuals in "mainstream" America contracted AIDS, concern about the disease and its potential for painful suffering and death grew. By the 1990s, AIDS was among the nation's leading killers, and large segments of the public were anxious to find a cure.[6]

Triggering Mechanism Factors in Tandem—and Not

For the most part, triggering events fail to reach or exceed the threshold for action required by the combination of scope, intensity, and timing. More times than not, the heterogeneous quality of American society dissipates the intensity of most claims on government. Likewise, rarely do sufficient quantities of individuals mobilize for change over a time span sufficiently long enough to generate enough momentum to change the boundaries of the public policy arena. In their study of the American public, Sidney Verba and Norman Nie note the possible reasons for the basically passive responses to most triggering mechanisms. They find that the individual agendas of citizens are fantastically varied: "Each citizen has his own particular set of problems and concerns [which] are close to his own life space, involving job, family, house. Or, if what concerns him is more general—war, high prices, the quality of schools, traffic problems, property taxes—there remains an almost infinite variety of personal sets of public issues."[7] Given changing combinations of attitudes and issues, it is the exception rather than the rule for public opinion to coalesce around a triggering mechanism for any length of time.

Still, political scientists differ on whether people are more or less disposed by the events around them to press the political system for change. Writing about the 1994 midterm national election, Clyde Wilcox concluded, "First, the public is generally dissatisfied with the way government works. Second, it wants to reduce the size of government, primarily through cuts in spending." Wilcox points to the decisive Republican victory as an example of an engaged electorate.[8] Yet, another recent analysis of political behavior by Steven Rosenstone and John Mark Hansen argues that a "waning sense of political efficacy has caused citizens to disengage massively from politics and elections."[9] Ironically, both assessments may be true, in the sense that those who vote have been motivated to move in another direction, although the numbers of those committed to the process are fewer than ever. Either way, social science experts acknowledge a relationship between issue involvement and the demand for political action.

Scope, intensity, and timing explain the impact of triggering mechanisms on the public policy making process. To the extent that these three factors become more pronounced, the influence of the triggering event becomes more important in formulation of issues for the public agenda. These three factors may interact in various strengths; their sum total of entanglement will produce a more or less powerful inducement for political action.

Figure 2.1 demonstrates the interaction among scope, intensity, and timing, and the relative strengths of the triggering mechanisms that are yielded from these relationships. Each of the cases presented in Figure 2.1 reveals a different combination of characteristics.

Triggering mechanisms constitute linkage between the perception of a problem and the demand for political action. They occur at a point when the psychological elasticity between what *is* and what *should be* is stretched out of its usual shape. Robert Lineberry refers to this juncture as the moment when sufficient numbers of people become cognizant of a performance gap and realize that "something is wrong

Figure 2.1 **Triggering Mechanism Components: Scope, Intensity, and Timing** (selected case studies)

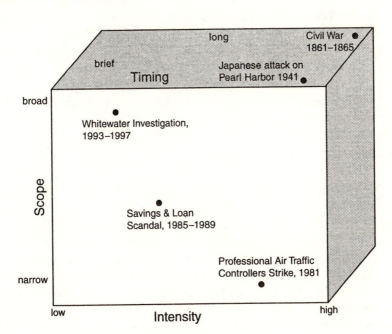

with present policy, . . . that ongoing institutions are not resolving or ameliorating problems they are supposed to deal with."[10] Combined, scope, intensity, and timing provide the necessary ingredients for the triggering mechanism component.

Categories of Triggering Mechanisms

As potential forerunners to public policies, triggering mechanisms emerge from two different environments: internal (domestic) and external (foreign). Internal events are discussed in the section immediately below, while external triggering mechanisms are addressed in the section that follows.

For the most part, Americans do not involve themselves in the machinations of foreign policy. The issues, events, and consequences of activities abroad are rarely perceived as important enough to be incorporated into daily routines. Even policy questions regarding national security are generally viewed by most American citizens in the context of economic rather than military battles.[11] This is not to say that Americans ignore foreign policy if they perceive a serious threat to the status quo, as demonstrated by the extent of anxiety over the Vietnam War and, more recently, the Persian Gulf conflict. Nevertheless, these experiences rarely tend to overshadow traditional domestic issues for long periods of time.[12] Given our inward issue orientation and budgetary commitments, it stands to reason that most triggering mechanisms impact the domestic arena.

Internal Triggering Mechanisms

Critical events are not always neatly packaged for political analysis. For example, an economic disaster may occur simultaneously with social change, or social change may accompany a technological transformation, sometimes making it difficult to place a single event or a series of events into a particular category. That caveat aside, there are five critical points of origin for internal triggering mechanisms: natural catastrophes, economic calamities, technological breakthroughs, ecological shifts, and social evolution. These sources serve as the wellsprings of triggering mechanisms and the public policies that may follow as a result of their occurrences.

Natural Catastrophes

Natural catastrophes occur independently of activities undertaken by individuals or governments. Although not political in nature, these events and their consequences may alter political values and priorities. Thus, when natural catastrophes take place, their suddenness and the subsequent chains of events can have major disruptive impacts on populations, social structures, and economies.

It is difficult to imagine that natural catastrophes could serve as triggering mechanisms in a nation such as the United States, where 97 percent of the population lives in urban or suburban environments. Inasmuch as we control electric power, the flow of water, indoor temperatures, and many other aspects of our daily existence, it seems unlikely that any environmental devastation would be so massive as to trigger the demand for public policy response. Many disastrous incidents—hurricanes, floods, and earthquakes, to name a few—occur with great frequency. Yet, in light of their generally localized impacts, most of the time, the scopes of these triggering events tend to be rather narrow, and the lengths of their disruptions to everyday life are fairly brief.

The 1994 Northridge earthquake in California was a natural catastrophe with profound consequences for the region, the state, and the nation. More than a simple temblor, the massive quake occurred in a densely populated area of Los Angeles and registered 6.4 on the 1–10 Richter scale. Immediately, virtually the entire region became hostage to nature, as many major highways collapsed or otherwise became inoperable. More than fifty people lost their lives, hundreds of buildings were declared unsafe, and tens of thousands of residents were displaced from their homes for several weeks and more. On another level, the area's economy, already ravaged from recession and the dramatic reduction of its highly valued defense/aerospace industry, sunk to a new level of collective despair.

The Northridge earthquake triggered immediate response from the national government's Federal Emergency Management Agency (FEMA), which dispatched 2,450 representatives to the area with various financial rescue packages and emergency planning programs for more than 500,000 applicants. Within two days of the event, President Bill Clinton toured the area and promised immediate assistance. Following the president's lead, federal bureaucrats waived the usual matching provisions for various grant-in-aid requirements. Shortly thereafter, Congress passed an $8 billion relief package, with funds directed for highway repairs, environmental protection, small business loans and grants, and individual citizen assistance. The infusion of funds not only helped with recovery from the earthquake but also assisted with general economic repair. More than 20,000 jobs were added to the local economy, as the area climbed out of its worst decline in sixty years.[13]

Because of its extensive scope, the Northridge quake precipitated massive federal government response. This action occurred despite the fact that national policy makers were hamstrung by serious demands to balance the federal budget without assuming any other major expenditures. Nevertheless, national priorities were restructured in response to the natural catastrophe.

Economic Calamities

Economic events interface with the social and political arenas of life. Changes in employment or productivity, for example, lead to shifts in earning and purchasing power of individuals and businesses alike; these, in turn, may generate new conditions in the political environment. This is not to suggest that economic events are solely "independent" variables, or the factors that only cause change. Sometimes, new public policies promote alterations in the economy, rearranging the status quo in their aftermath. When new policies are formulated, interested parties often have the opportunity to shape such policies in advance. But when economic calamities occur, their suddenness often gives affected parties little advance notice.

The collapse of the banking industry in the early 1980s exemplifies the extent to which economic demise can affect society and trigger the demand for change. During the 1960s and 1970s, several factors converged to place the industry under siege. Financing of the Vietnam War, a rapid Cold War defense buildup, soaring energy prices, and expanded domestic spending programs occurred year after year, with little effort to balance income and spending patterns. If anything, periodic tax cuts by national policy makers only exacerbated pressures on the economy.[14] Combined, these events set the stage for massive inflation.

By 1980, inflation was rampant in the United States. During this year alone, the prime rate (the percentage charged by banks for loans to their largest and most favored customers) changed forty-two times and fluctuated wildly between 11 and 21.5 percent. Banks and savings and loans were caught between a rock and a hard place. On the one hand, customers were paying interest rates on mortgages considerably less than the rates that the money institutions were paying to borrow. On the other hand, financial institutions were paying interest rates in the 5 percent range during this period, leaving investors with disappearing principles.

During the same period, national legislation deregulated much of the banking industry, with the intent of increasing competition among financial institutions. With new rules in place, many individuals and companies with little banking experience attempted to break into the industry with "get-rich-quick" schemes for investors. In some cases, the new opportunities were based on unnecessary risk; in other cases, they were just plain fraudulant.

In 1982, an Oklahoma bank failed. Shortly thereafter, Continental of Illinois, the nation's eighth largest bank, also closed its doors, leading to a "run" by investors on numerous banks and savings and loans throughout the country. In each case involving a federally chartered or state-chartered bank, investors recovered as much as $100,000 from the Federal Deposit Insurance Corporation (FDIC) and other similar agencies. Within a decade, more than 1,200 banks and savings and loans were declared insolvent, leaving the U.S. government on the hook for $400 billion. But in many instances, "nonbank" banks—new financial institutions that acted like banks—suffered insititutional bankruptcies that cost investors billions of unrecoverable dollars.[15]

But the financial crisis buck did not stop with the federal government as much as it passed through to taxpayers who, ultimately, had to foot the bill through more taxes or higher interest on the national debt. And how much was it? Enough to cost each American family the equivalent of $20 per month for the next thirty years![16] As a result of these events, critics demanded (and received) new government reforms.

Technological Breakthroughs

Technology provides a continuous stream of change for society, and often with profound repercussions. The consequences from technological developments can literally alter relationships between individuals, corporations, and even nations.

Consider the automobile. When Henry Ford assembled a staff of 125 men at his factory in 1903, he created a series of other conditions as well. Ford needed a large pool of available labor; he also required sizable quantities of steel, rubber, electricity, and resources from other support industries. As a result of the technological breakthroughs related to mass production of automobiles, the political system was bombarded with new challenges regarding highway development, petroleum acquisition, air pollution, proper working conditions, and numerous other issues.

Put simply, technological breakthroughs affect much more than the creation of products. Since economic, social, and political environments are intertwined, technological breakthroughs are likely to trigger adjustments throughout society. As one authority notes, "technology exacts its costs not only in energy demand [for the actual change] but also upon the patterns of human behavior and institutional arrangements necessary to enable technology to work in socially or ecologically desirable ways."[17] The conflicts that result from altered behavior patterns and institutional responses quickly transfer to the political environment.

The inventions of television and the computer are two technical breakthroughs that have had immense impacts on individual lives and public policies. With the development of television in the 1940s, mass communication in the United States was elevated to an entirely new level of exchange. Individuals in the most remote regions of the country could be informed of happenings in Washington, across the world, or in outer space. Televised presidential debates, wars in distant lands, and even such events as the murder trial of noted sports celebrity O.J. Simpson are now brought into our homes with the flick of a switch.

The proliferation of computers represents another juncture in history where technology has changed the way we live. From computer-aided design (CAD) techniques to the personal computer, this technology has introduced new levels of efficiency, knowledge, and information transfer into virtually every level of society. Because of its capacity to process information quickly and accurately, the computer and the technological revolution have redefined the limits of what society can do.[18] Surgeries, missile designs, and artificial life are but a few of the areas that have undergone fundamental evolution because of the computer.

Far from bringing about benign change, technology has fostered wholesale alternations in American society. On repeated occasions, it has triggered awareness and new directions in issue areas which otherwise might have remained in a different condition.

Ecological Shifts

Many of the resources most necessary to human survival exist only in finite quantities and are vulnerable to depletion. In some countries, land has been tilled and retilled to the point of poor productivity. In other countries, water has not always been available in required quantities for agricultural functions. Worldwide, the consumption of oil has increased faster than the ability to find new petroleum or to discover substitute energy sources. Some of the most pressing contemporary ecological problems stem from a world population explosion that shows little sign of controlled growth. Other concerns are associated with the effects of technology on the biological, physical, and chemical environments.

Shifts in the ecological balance have potentially widespread impacts as triggering mechanisms. Whether the problem is local or transnational in scope, the loss or depletion of resources can become critical to the future distribution of goods and values. Lynton Caldwell, a noted authority on environmental politics, reasons that "civilization" is defined in part by the ways and extent to which people alter their natural conditions.[19] In the course of managing our environments, we run the risk of both ecological change and potential redistribution of critical resources. Thus, the balance of nature and political life are closely intertwined.

Rarely does ecological change take place strictly under its own momentum. The glacier age and the eventual burnout of the earth's sun constitute two such purely natural environmental events. Such situations are likely to be dramatic because they demonstrate that there are times when humankind cannot control its destiny. Most of the time, however, ecological shifts happen slowly in response to human activity which, at least at the time, is not perceived as problematic. The discovery of an ecological shift may be shocking enough to trigger public reactions and, hence, to raise previously unconsidered public policy issues.

The ecological changes resulting from water pollution have led to concern and political change. Water, of course, is basic to human survival; it is a means of travel as well as a foundation for the food chain. With increases in industrialization and population during the twentieth century, many critical functions of water have been threatened. As a source of food, Lake Erie was declared "dead" during the 1960s because of pollution. Even more dramatic has been the havoc wreaked by "acid rain" on large Canadian and American populations and their water supplies, thereby jeopardizing hundreds of plant and animal species.[20]

More recently, the world has been troubled by an international ecological shift, the depletion of the ozone layer. This invisible blanket around the earth has served to shelter people from many of the sun's harmful ultraviolet rays, the excessive exposure to which can cause skin cancer. By the late 1980s, numerous studies confirmed what many had earlier speculated—namely, that "holes" had developed in the ozone layer because of the large amount of chlorofluorocarbons (CFCs) that had been pumped into the air from a variety of sources in the industrialized world. Since then, these nations have developed substitutes, although deterioration continues, albeit at a much slower pace.

Ecological shifts demonstrate the extent to which unusually powerful forces can disrupt life's most basic staples. They also show the difficulties that nations face when, in order to solve these problems, they must alter their priorities for the good of the international community.

Social Evolution

Social evolution takes place as large sectors of society alter attitudes toward values, behavior, and government obligations. Such changes are hard to detect because of the many factors that promote stability among the public and thereby discourage change. American citizens are socialized at an early age, and are taught that compromise is preferable to conflict and cooperation is more desirable than rebellion. Indeed, our political culture is framed in large part by a series of attitudes that encourages obedience to authority over excessive dissent.[21] Robert Eyestone observes that "many social problems in the United States are endemic, or least remarkably resistant to solution. Problems under the general headings of war, poverty, and ethnic groups relations fall into this category."[22] These dilemmas, then, are not passing in nature; rather, they seem permanent fixtures in the American constellation of ideas and values.

Despite long-standing inertia that mitigates against fundamental change, there are those points in history at which values and events converge to push society in new directions and, hence, to rearrange the social fabric. As a result of these changes, the boundaries of acceptable political action assume new dimensions.

Few examples of social evolution have been as sweeping as the women's rights movement. Similar to other changes of great impact, this concept gradually has gained support over its lengthy, stormy history. While the Nineteenth Amendment gave women constitutional equality "on paper," critics charged that the new guarantees were blunted by a series of barriers constructed in the private sector as well as by government institutions. Yet, demands for equal treatment with men fell on deaf ears until a series of other long-term changes transpired. Declining birthrates, fewer marriages, larger numbers of female college graduates, and greater participation in the workforce by women were all factors responsible in the movement to rethink women's status in social, economic, and political systems.[23] These changed attitudes toward women crystallized in the 1960s and 1970s; more important, they set the stage for policy changes and increased female clout in the political process.

The expansion of their roles in American society triggered women's demands for a larger share of society's benefits. But, much as other discriminated groups did, women suffered profound economic deprivation.[24] Armed with ammunition of inequity, advocates pursued legislation designed to overcome income disparities. Their quest met with some success. In 1974, the Equal Credit Opportunity Act was passed, national legislation that banned credit discrimination on the basis of gender. The women's movement's momentum slowed somewhat when three-fourths of the states failed to approve a proposed equal rights amendment during the late 1970s. Nevertheless, the "equal pay for comparable work" question was partially resolved in 1981. At that time, the U.S. Supreme Court ruled that women who receive lower salaries than men may file suit against their employers for sex discrimination—even if their work assignments are not identical—on the assumption that some job skills are comparable. In 1988, the Court ruled that the exclusion of women from private social clubs denied them the opportunity to "network" in ways similar to males.[25] It was not until 1996 that the Court declared that university military academies must admit women into their programs.

Today, women still earn less than two-thirds of their male counterparts, although this figure is much higher than even a decade ago, when they averaged only half. Even in employment, however, the data suggests mixed results. In the highest ranks of industry, comparably trained women executives earn 70 cents for every dollar earned by men. One recent study actually shows a larger wage gap at the top in 1993, as compared to a decade earlier.[26]

In the electoral arena, women have achieved near parity in several state legislatures, with several elected to governorships. At the national level, their numbers have tripled over the past twenty years, and yet only a small fraction of those elected to the U.S. Senate and House of Representatives are women. All factors considered, the rising consciousness of women as equals has triggered debate on these political issues and has influenced subsequent policy changes. Nowhere has this leadership been more evident than with the passage of the Family Leave Act of 1993, a law that grants unpaid twelve-week leaves for workers in cases of family illness or after childbirth, and with increased congressional support for research on women's health issues.

External Triggering Mechanisms

Foreign policy is the determination of how one country acts toward another. Exchanges of commerce, ideas, technologies, and violence are some of the more important aspects of foreign policy. Throughout the twentieth century, the interaction among nations has increased tremendously. Whereas oceans, mountains, and other natural barriers once limited exchanges between nations, modern technologies have condensed the world to dimensions so small that a satellite can circle it in less than ninety minutes. It is this sense of shrinkage that gives new importance to external events. Given the increasing ability of nations to overcome once-formidable physical barriers, external events often act as triggering mechanisms for some of the most explosive issues and policy activities.

Like their internal counterparts, external events create issues that appear on the public agenda. Although the scope may be such that only two or three of the world's nations are involved initially, the intensity of these triggering mechanisms is generally high. Meanwhile, the time horizon may be incredibly brief, if volatile. Moreover, the "spillover" possibilities are endless even for those countries not directly involved in a conflict. Inasmuch as the United States is a nation of unusual global involvement, it is commonly affected by external triggering mechanisms regardless of the country for which they are intended.

Four major categories of external events trigger new policy issues for domestic consideration: acts of war, indirect conflicts, economic confrontation, and the growth of weaponry. These are examined individually in the sections below.

Acts of War

The military violation of one nation by another represents the most blatant example of an external triggering mechanism. Even if nations are not engaged in conflict, they are most likely to be participants in activities related to conflict. Hans Morganthau once wrote that virtually all "nations active in international politics are continuously preparing for, actively involved in, or recovering from organized violence in the form of war."[27] If the nuclear age has divided the world into military "haves" and "have-nots," it has not reduced the opportunity for any one nation to engage another in war. Even the end of the Cold

War has not eliminated the possibility of one nation's pursuing another. Unlike other nations in the world community, the United States has been affected by relatively few acts of war. However, the events leading to World War II represent a vivid account of war as a triggering mechanism for public reaction. As a result of the Japanese surprise attack on American soil in 1941, American attitudes toward participation in the international conflict reversed from reluctant involvement to immediate participation. The unanticipated event at Pearl Harbor triggered an entire series of questions that brought immediate responses. The event was broad in scope and high in intensity. Although the activity lasted but a few hours, the changes in American approach were massive. This event stands as a clear-cut example of how an external event can mobilize demand for domestic response.

Few triggering events have affected the public policy process with either the clarity or the totality of World War II. More commonly, the intentions behind foreign policy moves are difficult to discover, making interpretation a difficult task for the policy analyst. Particularly when war is a possibility, the lack of clear-cut alternatives can be a liability for a nation responding to a threat. Under these circumstances, external triggering events are open to conflicting assessments at home due to "second guessing" about motives; more times than not, this lack of clarity contributes to an atmosphere of domestic confusion, if not rancor.

The Persian Gulf conflict of 1990–91 exemplifies a war that developed out of unusual conditions. In this action, unlike World War II, the United States was not attacked directly by another nation; instead, on August 2, 1990, the United States as well as the rest of the community of nations witnessed an Iraqi assault on Kuwait, its neighbor to the south. Upon taking control of the Kuwaiti territory, Iraqi President Saddam Hussein announced annexation of the area as Iraq's nineteenth province.

Although the United States was not an immediate party to the military struggle, American leaders contended that the Iraqi invasion of Kuwait was illegal, immoral, and subject to rebuke. In addition, because 70 percent of the world's petroleum reserves are found in the Middle East, many observers feared that the warfare would bring about instability in the always-precarious oil industry.

At first, President George Bush, acting on a request from the exiled leaders from Kuwait, promised that American ships would intercept all products entering and leaving Iraq.[28] But bearing in mind the sovereignty issues and concerns of many other nations in the area, representatives from the United States joined with other nations to express their anger before the Security Council, a fifteen-member body of the United Nations. After several days of debate, the Security Council ordered Iraq to leave Kuwait by January 15, 1991, or face international reprisals. When Iraqi forces failed to withdraw by this date, the Security Council authorized a consortium of nations led by the United States to take the military actions necessary to force Iraqi withdrawal.[29] Between January 15 and March 1991, American air power and 500,000 U.S. troops led twenty-eight nations in an intensive assault on Iraqi troops and military facilities, with Hussein accepting United Nations terms for peace on April 4, 1991.[30]

The end of the Cold War may have limited the number of superpowers, but the ability of one nation to harm another remains widespread. With increased access of many nations to nuclear capabilities, it has become relatively easy for one nation to harm another. When the Union of Soviet Socialist Republics (USSR) disintegrated into thirteen autonomous republics in 1991, for example, Ukraine, Kazakhstan, and Belarus suddenly became nuclear powers overnight by virtue of the arsenals on their lands. The selling of nuclear technology by some nations to others also has made the world a much more dangerous place than it was a decade ago, when the superpowers kept most of the technology within their control. Such conditions increase not only the possibility of war but the probability of accidents.

Indirect Conflicts

In addition to the overt struggles between nations, the precipitation of conflict may affect the policy patterns of other parties as well. When this development occurs, the area of conflict grows and stakes increase. Furthermore, the involvement of additional nations in a military conflict invites additional opportunities for unexpected events to take place.

The civil war in Bosnia exemplifies not only a tragedy befalling a young nation, but a struggle for influence among several neighboring countries, and among nations throughout the world. Bosnia, one of several nations created from the former Yugoslavia, suffered from strife among Greek Orthodox Serbs, Muslims, and Roman Catholic Croats. Yet, aside from its obvious religious overtones, the Bosnian civil war also was an armed conflict based upon historical, ethnic, and religious layers of hostility. In addition, Russia, Iraq, and the United States have all worked behind the scenes to effect outcomes favorable to their interests. In 1995, President Clinton upped the ante in the Bosnian struggle by deploying 20,000 American troops for peace-keeping purposes related to the separation of the parties and organization of a presidential election in the war-torn nation. Clinton's move sparked anger from some nations and relief from others. And while his effort no doubt brought about a major reduction of violence, Clinton's decision also brought the United States perilously close to participation in the conflict. Nevertheless, Bosnian elections were held successfully in September 1996, thereby allowing Clinton to keep the U.S. role to a minimum while restoring peace, albeit fragile, in the region.

As we prepare to enter a new millennium, several areas of the world remain in turmoil because of smoldering tensions between nations. Among them:

- *India and Pakistan.* Most experts concede that both India and Pakistan have nuclear weapons as components of their military arsenals. Within the past decade, the two have clashed over borders, and their disputes remain unresolved.
- *Iran and Iraq.* Prior to its invasion of Kuwait in 1990, Iraq had been at war with Iran for a decade. Since the Persian Gulf War, Iran has stepped up its efforts to purchase nuclear technology from Russia and Kazakhstan. Meanwhile, Iraq, many observers believe, has much of its nuclear program intact.
- *North Korea and China.* The struggle for military dominance between the Asian powers has implications for South Korea, Japan, and the United States, among others. South Korea has hinted that it may develop a nuclear self-defense, while the United States has struggled over how much nuclear and computer technology it should sell to China.[31]
- *Russia and Chechnia.* The war between Russia and an area that was once a small part of the Soviet Union carries not only the risk of involvement by nearby nations but the potential for increased turmoil within Russia itself.

Along with the prominent examples cited above, skirmishes—some prominent, others not—persist throughout the globe. Africa has witnessed strife in Rwanda and Somalia; Japan and Russia continue to argue over ownership of the Kurile Islands; Indonesia and a half dozen other nations spar over the Spratly Islands; and the Middle East, while less volatile today than in the past, remains a hotbed of instability. Each of these centers of strife has the potential of blowing up beyond the boundaries of the combatants.

If anything, the end of the Cold War may have led to a more unstable world simply because nations are less dependent upon superpowers which, among other functions, once served to police their political satellites. With less discipline to check them, dissatisfied nations and their governments have the ability to turn on others and bring bystanders into unwanted confrontations. As Phil Williams writes, "in a world lacking the imperatives of bipolarity, alignments are likely to be much more fluid and more volatile than during the Cold War." As a result, what Williams describes as "rogue" states operate seemingly with reduced fears of repercussions.[32]

Economic Confrontations

On an abstract level, nations are defined by their sovereignty. They are independent units that assume responsibility for their own politics, military affairs, and economic organization. Practically speaking, however, nations exhibit a good deal of interdependence. For example, sovereign governments work together politically through the United Nations. From a military perspective, members of the North Atlantic Treaty Organization (NATO) exemplify the willingness of nations to defend each other in order to protect themselves (and the necessity for their doing so). In the economic realm, too, nations often find that, when they pool resources and needs, the collective benefits outweigh the costs. The European Economic Community (EEC), also known as the Common Market, is an example of a few countries that banded together to improve their collective lots at the cost of some national sovereignty.

Sometimes, nations do not work together with perfect synchronization. If, as some suggest, the "economic pie" of the world operates to the extent that one nation's gain is another nation's loss, then the sovereign economic policies that benefit some nations may bring harm to others. Certainly, a number of oil-importing countries have expressed these sentiments about their oil-exporting counterparts. Similar sentiments have been uttered by Third World, or "developing," nations who criticize industrialized countries for buying raw materials at low prices, only to sell them back as processed products for exorbitant profits.

Periodically, nations attempt to settle their differences through international bodies or at international conferences. Meetings at the United Nations, for example, have generated considerable support for restrictions on logging in countries that rely on trees as part of their ecosystems. On other occasions, efforts to reach agreement fail when a key party finds the terms unduly intrusive on its own interests. The 1992 Earth Summit in Rio de Janeiro constitutes a case in point. At this meeting, 153 nations signed an agreement that acknowledged national sovereignty over a nation's genetic resources, including medicines and drugs produced from endangered animals or plants. However, the United States declined to sign because of President Bush's claim that such an agreement would intrude on U.S. national interests.[33] Thus, the difference between what nations are willing to give and what they will gain may sometimes be too high a price to pay, partially negating the outcome of the general effort.

When one nation manages its economic policies in a manner harmful to another, economic confrontations often result. The second nation may suffer to the extent that its externally caused economic woes inspire economic or political rejoinders. Therefore, the economic policies of one nation can trigger retaliation from another, with deteriorated relations often the final outcome.

The United States has a long record as a leader in commerce and trade. It is not surprising, therefore, that when other countries attempt to undermine U.S. dominance, economic confrontations often result. Consider the uneven trade relationship between Japan and the United States. Since the late 1970s, Japan has enjoyed huge trade surpluses with the United States, particularly with respect to Japanese penetration of American markets in the areas of automobiles, computers, semiconductors, and telecommunications equipment.

Some economists have blamed the low level of American exports on the lack of American government incentives for U.S. companies attempting to do business abroad, while others have cast a wary eye at barriers put up by the Japanese government to foreign imports, thereby assuring profits for their own companies.[34] Ironically, while American politicians and business executives complained vehemently about Japanese protectionism, tariffs and quotas were imposed by the U.S. government on Japanese products ranging from metal cutting tools to low-priced tuna.[35] Similar to the justifications given by the Japanese, U.S. officials have designed these barriers as means to make foreign competition artificially expensive.

Recently, nations everywhere have reassessed the benefits of protectionism versus the costs of lost exports. In 1994, leaders of eighteen Pacific rim countries, including Japan and the United States, pledged to dismantle all trade barriers by the year 2020. In the same year, 124 nations ended seven years of talks as signatories to a treaty known as the General Agreement on Tariffs and Trade (GATT), a pact designed to slash tariffs by 40 percent, to cut subsidies, and to create new export international rules. Even at that, critics charged that much of the agreement was illusory and that new ways would be found to protect various industries before the treaty even took effect.[36]

New Weapons and the Balance of Power

Most analysts agree that if there is another world war, it will have a nuclear ring of finality, if not from direct assault, then from the massive radiation that will surely encircle the globe. Aside from the two atomic bombs dropped by the United States on Japan at the end of World War II, the community of nations has not experienced purposive nuclear disaster. However, whereas the United States enjoyed a virtual monopoly on nuclear technology fifty years ago, more than a dozen nations share this knowledge today. In addition, many nations now possess the means to develop and deploy arsenals of chemical and biological weapons, which can also wipe out large numbers of people.

The development of weapons has profound effects on the way that two or more nations respond to each other as well as on the entire international political system. As with most matters related to foreign affairs, weapons developments trigger reactions from relatively small sectors of society. Generally, only military and political elites are affected by military questions, although they may serve as opinion leaders for wider response on those rare occasions when segments of the public show interest.

If the scope of the public's knowledge concerning international weapons developments is rather narrow, the intensity of the issues can be substantial for those invested in the issue. An invention in one nation will automatically precipitate a reaction from an adversary. International relations authority Hans Morganthau once wrote that "the principal means . . . by which a nation endeavors with the power at its disposal to maintain or reestablish the balance of power are armaments. . . . The necessary corollary of the armaments race is a constantly increasing burden of military preparations . . . making for ever deepening fears, suspicions, and insecurity."[37] Far from being a policy decision with solely internal repercussions, a nation's commitment to new weapons may develop out of a "reactive linkage orientation" to the military policies of other nations.[38] Changes in weapons deployments and strategies have sweeping ramifications.

Two seemingly incompatible developments have occurred in the international weapons arena since the end of the Cold War. The first of these developments centers on the new role of the United States as the world's only remaining superpower. In an attempt to assure unrivaled primacy into the twenty-first century, the Department of Defense drafted a strategy to "prevent the re-emergence of a new rival." The core element of the plan rests on the United States' operating independently of the United Nations or other arrangements to keep control of the world order, while doing whatever is necessary to keep other nations from acquiring weapons of mass destruction.[39]

The second development concerns the ever-widening availability of weapons by producers to new, eager consumers, many of which are Third World or developing nations. Russia, for example, has sold nuclear materials and/or technologies to Iran; Germany has made available sophisticated weaponry to Indonesia; Great Britain has provided heat-seeking image devices for Pakistan; and the list goes on and on.[40] Not to be lost in the discussion is the role of the United States, which, despite the desire to maintain hegemony, has emerged as the most prolific arms supplier. In 1993, for example, the United States accounted for almost 60 percent of weapons sales to Third World countries, making it the world's largest arms dealer.[41] Regardless of the distributor, each sale of arms increases the opportunity for one nation to ravage another, not to mention the possibility of accidental use.

Forty years ago, then-Professor (later Secretary of State) Henry Kissinger observed that "in addition to the psychological and political problems, the technological race makes it difficult to negotiate a control plan [for international peace safeguards]. For the rate of technology has outstripped the pace of diplomatic negotiations."[42] The perfection of germ warfare and sophisticated military space satellites—all accomplished in the name of defense—have left the world's population in a precarious state of vulnerability.

External Triggering Events and Domestic Repercussions

The discussion thus far has treated external and internal triggering mechanisms as separate phenomena. Internal triggering events commonly stir the public conscience on issues relative to the domestic sphere. With respect to foreign-inspired triggering events, the results are equally predictable: external events stimulate domestic responses for the primary purpose of coping with foreign policy issues. In either situation, the focus of public reply is determined by the origin of the triggering mechanism.

Circumstances sometimes prevail in which, under unique conditions, external triggering mechanisms bring about responses for a nation's domestic agenda only. In these particular cases, new domestic issues are raised by international events that the affected nation has little ability to control or change, and political reaction tends to center on domestic objectives.

The persistence of international terrorism and the development of the French birth control drug RU-486 are two examples of external events that have impacted U.S. domestic policies. International terrorism was long considered a "problem" abroad much more than an issue at home. Skyjackings over international waters and bombings abroad, while despised by U.S. leaders, were viewed as issues that were largely the responsibility of other nations. U.S. attitudes changed in 1993, after Muslim fundamentalists bombed the New York International Trade Center, causing dozens of deaths and injuries.

In the case of RU-486, the development of a simple set of "morning-after" pills in France enables a women to end the possibility of any pregnancy immediately after intercourse and long before any concern about a viable fetus; the new pill is also touted for its ability to fight other maladies suffered by women. Though popular in Europe and Asia, RU-486 has precipitated a huge public policy debate in the United States on the grounds that the drug might interfere with the "right to life." Although the Bush administration prevented use of the RU-486 in the United States, the Clinton administration gave the Food and Drug Administration (FDA) permission to test the pill for nonpregnancy possibilities, leading to limited approval in 1996 and a new round of protests from the Right to Life movement.

The linkage between external events and domestic impacts point to the extent to which sovereign nations are dependent upon international affairs. While countries may attempt to isolate themselves from distasteful or controversial developments abroad, the fact remains that external-internal linkages can result in the transformation of external developments into domestic issues.

Triggering Mechanisms—Wellsprings of Public Policy

Triggering mechanisms are only as important as the responses they generate. Given a variety of pressures—both domestic and international—at any point in time, it is difficult to project which occurrences are likely to assume the importance of triggering events. Those phenomena relating to change alone do not necessarily fall into the triggering mechanism category. If events gently nudge society into a new direction without a sense of disorientation or anxiety, then such developments will evolve without the triggering event as a public policy stimulus. Moreover, if society accepts upheavals as natural or routine, then their impact as triggering mechanisms will be minimal as well. These disclaimers notwithstanding, it is important to remember that *triggering mechanisms are the catalysts for pressures which, in turn, lead to demands for new or changed public policies.*

Scope, intensity, and the timing associated with triggering mechanisms help to determine the impact of a given event on public values. But, in many instances, an event will not shake out as predicted. For example, despite the murders, rapes, and detentions of more than 100,000 people in Bosnia, Americans have been almost blasé about the horror in Central Europe; accordingly, President Clinton's late decision to deploy 20,000 peacekeeping troops drew more scorn than applause. Similarly, the savings and loan scandal of the late 1980s and the early 1990s failed to stir much nationwide concern, despite the fact that the debacle cost American taxpayers more than $500 billion. Then again, there are times when the triggering mechanism components collide in such a manner as to spark almost instant public policy. The bombing of the Murrah Federal Building in Oklahoma City in 1995, for example, triggered a near-instant response from President Clinton and Congress in the form of strengthened antiterrorism legislation.

Although triggering mechanisms may not develop as anticipated, occasionally such events generate a momentum of their own that expands scope and intensity over a prolonged period of time. In these cases, the triggering mechanism becomes the stimulus for subsequent events, almost as an earthquake provokes aftershocks. When the Watergate affair was first reported in 1972, President Nixon referred to it as a "third-rate burglary." The nation, caught between the dazzle of a presidential election campaign and the tragedy of Vietnam, seemed all too anxious to agree. Yet, subsequent events in the forms of investigations, trials, and public confessions gave new weight to Watergate as a defining moment in American politics. President Nixon resigned in the face of certain impeachment and near-certain conviction over his management of and role in the issue. Thus, the seemingly unimportant triggering event of Watergate ultimately led to a much more important political response—the resignation of Richard Nixon from the presidency.

Triggering mechanisms are the starting points for public policy questions. Their occurrences are difficult to anticipate, while their impacts on the public are equally unpredictable. Aside from the uncertainties discussed above, triggering mechanisms should be appreciated for their role in organizing public policy issues that emerge on the public agenda. They are the crucial forerunners of the public policy making process.

Questions for Further Thought

1. Triggering mechanisms have been described as the wellsprings of public policy. Explain the linkages in this relationship.

2. What do scope, intensity, and timing tell us about triggering mechanisms? How do they combine to create issues for the public agenda?

3. Distinguish internal triggering mechanisms from external triggering mechanisms. In what ways do they impact on each other? How do they differ in their impacts of society and public policy makers?

Suggested Reading

Crotty, William, ed., *Post–Cold War Policy* (Chicago: Nelson-Hall, 1995).

Eyestone, Robert, *From Issues to Public Policy* (New York: John Wiley and Sons, 1978).

Hamilton, Edward K, ed., *America's Global Interests* (New York: W.W. Norton, 1989).

Nock, Steven L., and Paul W. Kingston, *The Sociology of Public Issues* (Belmont, CA: Wadsworth, 1990).

Rosenstone, Steven J., and John Mark Hansen, *Mobilization, Participation and Democracy in America* (New York: Macmillan, 1993).

Thobaben, Robert G., Donna M. Schlagheck, and Charles Funderburk, *Issues in American Political Life,* 2d ed. (Englewood Cliffs, NJ: Prentice-Hall, 1995).

3 THE PUBLIC AGENDA: FOCAL POINT FOR POLICY DECISIONS

Like daily newspaper headlines, the issues challenging government leaders change by the day. Whereas most problems tend to be absorbed into everyday life with little consequence, other occurrences in the economic, social, and technological spheres capture public concern in varying degrees. These questions become part of the *public agenda, a political barometer of the most sensitive problems which have reached the attention of policy makers for management and disposition.*

As with a barometer that reacts to different climatological conditions, the public agenda changes as public priorities and values shift. Like the policy decisions that emerge in its wake, the public agenda possesses a dynamic presence. Thus, Robert Eyestone concludes, the combination of problems confronting modern society is hardly static in quantity or quality.[1] Some problems are a "one-time" phenomenon: they reach the public agenda, are solved by policy makers, and never reappear. Other problems are open-ended in nature. An issue may be so complicated or so divisive that little other than temporary patchwork can be applied, leaving the distinct impression among participants that the issue will reemerge at another time. In summary, the public agenda is a changing collection of major issues, often unpredictable and volatile, awaiting action by policy makers.

The relationship between triggering mechanisms and the public agenda comprises powerful linkage for the policy making process. After triggering mechanisms catapult once private or undiscovered matters into public view, these questions join other issues which are ongoing public agenda items. Grouped together, these issues awaiting response by public policy makers generally are in various stages of resolution, stalemate, or decomposition. Whether such questions are placed before a local school board or the U.S. Congress, virtually all government entities deal with an agenda full of unresolved matters.

In this chapter, we will address the public agenda from several perspectives. First, as public policy analysts, we must identify the sources of agenda building, that is, the people who bring the message to policy makers. Some messengers—elected officials, for example—are fairly visible to the public. Other agenda-building agents are considerably less noticeable to the public eye, but effective nonetheless. In addition, some agenda builders are more successful than others because of their public exposure, political clout, or official responsibilities in the public policy making arena. It is one thing for an obscure bureaucrat to write an esoteric treatise about the addictive potential of tobacco; it is quite another for the Director of the Food and Drug Administration to articulate the same claim before the House of Representatives Health and Labor Committee, while flanked by a dozen television cameras. Awareness of those responsible for organization of the public agenda allows us a more comprehensive understanding of the myriad sources of pressure and policy change.

Second, we will explore the various symbolic and substantive issues that constitute the public agenda. Symbolic issues evoke decisions on political values, while substantive issues deal with the allocation of government resources. Such categorizations help clarify the claims on government; they also give insight into the possibilities for resolving controversial issues through new public policies. If the issue is symbolic, it may be satisfied with a proclamation or statement of intent, leaving the larger questions unaddressed. However, the more substantive an issue becomes, the more imperative it is for policy makers to satisfy competing interests and goals. Given a complex issue, policy makers' abilities to decide outcomes may be sorely tested and subjected to pressures from many directions.

Third, we will examine the difficulties of organizing and reorganizing the public agenda. As the values of public and policy makers change, so do their definitions of the troublesome problems facing them. Of course, some issues have a perennial quality. At the same time, new questions may be triggered unexpectedly at a moment's notice. Under some conditions, such as a troubled economy, the surge of new issues over a short time span may not only be dramatic, but test the limits of the political system. Thus, the public agenda shifts like a series of snapshots taken in rapidly changing scenery: The sights at one moment may be considerably different from those observed at another. The difficulty of separating issues from nonissues compounds the public agenda puzzle. When examining agenda components, the question is often asked, to what extent are the publicly expressed problems the *real* problems of society? Are there nonissues that have been suppressed from public exposure by private interests seeking to prevent open discussion? In order to fully assess the meaning of the public agenda, it is wise to determine whether the concerns of society actually have been expressed, heard, and accepted by policy makers as agenda items. Thus, we will discuss the concept of a "hidden agenda."

American society in the 1990s has witnessed an explosion of issues, leading to a crowded and disjointed public agenda. Representatives of countless interests believe that their problem is the one most in need of government attention. The list only seems to grow longer with each crisis. New demands for a range of social services, the shift from an industrial economic base to a service orientation, environmental concerns, equality issues, trade imbalances, and international competition are among the many problems that have surfaced and remained on the public agenda without resolution. U.S. public policy makers have both challenges and opportunities today as they have rarely had in the past. But, as William Crotty notes, "the outcome of the debate that has begun is anything but predictable."[2] Identifying the public agenda is one thing; resolving its issues is another altogether.

Agenda Builders

Aside from unpredictable issues that spring up from such events as natural catastrophes or military attacks, agenda building is a carefully orchestrated task. In general, the actors who bring potential policy issues into the public arena do so because they perceive the need to expose a political problem with the hope of altering an existing policy arrangement. In most cases, the public agenda develops out of the publicity and/or information that emanates from four basic sources: public officials, the mass media, interest groups, and the bureaucracy. These actors may work alone or in combination to place issues on the public agenda.

Public Officials

Elected public officials are perhaps the most obvious agents of the agenda building process. As policy makers themselves, these leaders may dramatize the importance of issues in an effort to mobilize public support and the cooperation of their colleagues in positions of authority. By virtue of their ability to make policy, public officials are in the unique position of placing issues on the public agenda and dealing with them. They are sought for their ability not only to express issues but to direct them through the policy making maze.

The President

No national leader reaches the American public in as many ways as the president. With the availability of modern communication techniques, presidents increasingly take their cases and issues to the people, through televised addresses, press conferences, and strategic meetings with carefully selected audiences. The strategy behind this effort is to cultivate public opinion as a means of gaining support. According to presidential scholar Samuel Kernell, the presidential prerogative of "going public" has increased steadily with each administration over the past half century.[3] As a result, the president tends to use the public as leverage against reluctant policy makers.

Setting the agenda can be both rewarding and frustrating for the chief executive, for his involvement in the process raises the stakes considerably. After Bill Clinton narrowly won the presidency in 1992, he attempted to seize the initiative in several policy areas, including gun control, approval of the North American Free Trade Agreement (NAFTA), and health reform. His tenacity may have made the difference in securing his narrow victories in the first two areas; but the president's inability to stay with a consistent message in the health arena may have hurt him more than any political damage done by the opposition.[4]

Clinton continued to set the agenda through his reelection effort in 1996, setting the tone with a focus on family issues, education, and twenty-first-century jobs. His approach to increased regulation of tobacco as a drug clearly distinguished the president from his opponent, Republican Bob Dole, leading the challenger, at one point, to dispute a sizable body of medical literature with his declaration that tobacco is not addictive.[5]

The Congress

Although attention has focused increasingly on the president, members of Congress are another set of well-known agents who help frame the public agenda. Legislative investigations, congressional committee hearings, and even individual members' inserts into the *Congressional Record* are all ways in which these individuals mold the public agenda.

A committee often will hold hearings on a given subject ostensibly so that it can uncover new information for public consumption, yet its real concerns may focus on an entirely different issue. Such was the case with the Republican minority on the Senate Judiciary Committee during the first two years of the Clinton administration. With nearly every nominee for a federal judicial post, committee Republicans pressed with aggressive challenges about their credentials. More than concern about any specific record, their goal was to demonstrate that the president was an individual much more liberal than his words.[6] Ironically, Senate Judiciary Committee Democrats had carried out much the same strategy in reverse during the Reagan and Bush presidencies. In each case, members pursued an agenda beyond the immediate issues before their committee.

The Courts

While the executive and the legislative branches are the most observable—and the most directly accountable—government agents responsible for shaping the public agenda, most institutions with nonelected government agents have been equally involved as agenda builders. In recent years, the courts have had active roles in placing issues before the public by virtue of what judges do or do not decide. Some of the more prominent and controversial areas include racial equality, the rights of criminal defendants, religious freedom, business regulation, issues relating to privacy, legislative reapportionment, and the distribution of power between the national and state governments.

Unlike the executive or legislative branches, judges place issues on the public agenda as a result of their decisions to examine, or not to examine, cases brought to their attention. That judges operate in this way stems from the requirements of Article III in the U.S. Constitution. Through their choices of justiciable topics, judges add issues to the public agenda. As a result, Henry Glick writes, "courts often create controversy."[7] This ability, moreover, extends from the highest centers of judicial activity in Washington to jurists at the state and local levels. Thus, although the nature of their offices precludes extensive direct public contact, judges play prominent roles in inserting questions onto the public agenda, particularly at the U.S. Supreme Court level.

Regulatory Agencies

Although generally not as visible as other policy making institutions, regulatory agencies may act as initiators of issues which, in turn, become part of the public agenda. The problems addressed by these government bodies can have a substantial impact on our economy and on our society. Moreover, simply deciding to discuss such issues as endangered species, computer software monopolies, or banking industry operations can capture the attention of policy makers and the public alike in policy areas that previously may not have had much visibility.

Some critics contend that while regulatory agencies are able to place critical issues before the public, they often lack the muscle to make policy changes.[8] The accuracy of this claim is likely to vary with the agency, its specific mandate, and its powers. Nevertheless, many regulatory agencies can make waves. Warren Kessler demonstrated this clout as Food and Drug Administration commissioner through his objections to false advertising and nonperforming products. His warnings were heeded by Congress in the form of subsequent committee hearings. Similarly, efforts by the Federal Communications Commission (FCC) to deal with cable regulation and deregulation have taken both the industry and consumers down an unpredictable path.[9]

Because regulatory agencies do not have as direct a relationship with the public as other policy making units have, their efforts to raise *and* act on policy questions sometimes are not as influential as other entities. Nevertheless, these organizations do have the ability to draw attention to key issues within their areas of jurisdiction.

The preceding discussion points to the multifaceted roles played by public officials in the agenda-building process. Most observers are familiar with the policy-formulating work that officials and leaders do, as we will discuss in chapter 4. But the agenda-developing characteristics of political actors tend to be overlooked and underrated. The ability to place issues on the agenda is as important as the ability to turn those issues into policy commitments.

Public Bureaucracy

The bureaucracy's function was once viewed as the neutral administration of law.[10] Conventional wisdom has long held that when politicians determine new rules, bureaucrats will manage them. This cut-and-dried view of bureaucracy has changed in light of the huge bureaucratic machines that exist today and that are guided to a large extent by political values. Although bureaucracies tend to have less policy making authority than official agents of change, they have the ability to affect the organization of the public agenda because of gridlock and gaps in other areas of the policy making arena.

Bureaucracy has come into its own as a power base. This development has been a consequence, in part, of the fragmented nature of authority in American politics and in American government. In the absence of centralized control, bureaucrats are often asked to step into the power vacuum to "make things work." Under such conditions, writes George Gordon, "it is not uncommon for public administrators to become significant 'players' in the political game, to assume a stance that is *not* neutral, [and] to take policy initiatives in small ways that nonetheless influence the long-term development of policies."[11] In other words, bureaucrats, because of their proximity to power, have the ability to place issues on the public agenda.

During the past half century, bureaucracies have enhanced their political positions by growth and function. With respect to size, about 2,800,000 civil servants (excluding 1,800,000 military personnel) worked for 150 different federal units of government in 1995—an increase of 1,600,000 over 1940, yet 300,000 less than 1980. They were divided among executive branch departments, independent regulatory agencies and bureaus, and government corporations.

The functional responsibilities of bureaucracies have also been transformed, with the increased complexity of government. Examination of contemporary bureaucracies by Kenneth Meier shows that they now engage in four critical political activities: regulatory policy, redistributive policy, distributive policy, and constituent policy. Acting in these capacities, Meier notes, bureaucracies "influence public policy through rule making, adjudication, law enforcement, program implementation, policy initiation, comments on proposed policy changes, and bureaucratic routines."[12]

Policy initiation in particular gives bureaucracies a vested interest in the agenda-setting process. When the Department of Health and Human Services announced new regulations for food labels in 1992, it made disclosure about nutritional value and content a question for the public agenda. But sometimes, a bureaucracy can find itself in hot water when it broaches a subject that becomes a nonissue. Thus, when the Environmental Protection Agency (EPA) sounded the alarm over the toxicity of the chemical dioxin in the early 1980s, a full decade went by before the agency recanted its concerns.[13]

In light of their multifaceted role in the policy process, bureaucracies have become increasingly active in the formulation of public questions. Because of their longevity relative to other policy makers, bureaucrats can wield considerable influence. Elected officials hold power only as long as they retain their offices; public bureaucrats tend to have lengthy periods of employment. Thus, the long-term influence of bureaucrats on the public agenda can be substantial.

The Media

The media, both print and electronic, have a long-standing reputation for placing issues on the public agenda. News reports raise the awareness of both policy makers and their constituents. Roger Cobb and Charles Elder refer to this activity as *arousal*: "Dependence on the media for spreading [issues] to the larger public increases with the expanding scope of conflict. . . . Arousal feeds on itself and tends to snowball. When the media takes an interest in a situation, they usually follow up on it, generating greater and greater attention and concern."[14] The media are useful not only as discovery mechanisms of public matters, but also as catalysts for what E.E. Schnattschneider once described as the "socialization of conflict."[15] By transforming a once-private question into a public issue, media agents expand the size of the audience and, thus, alter the dynamics of the policy making process.

In recent years the media have highlighted a number of events which, as a result of the media's efforts, were incorporated into the public agenda. Press reports on scandals such as the Watergate affair, the Iran-Contra cover-up and the savings and loan industry debacle not only heightened public awareness, but led to congressional hearings; trials and, in some cases, convictions; as well as new laws. Members of the media have also exposed glaring weaknesses in existing laws and regulations. Other recent media efforts have drawn attention to war atrocities in Bosnia, Somalia, and Haiti; to human rights problems at home and abroad; to poverty in America; to government waste; and to deceptive advertising claims made by drug producers, tobacco companies, and chemical manufacturers.[16]

Not all media revelations become part of the public agenda. Consider the changes associated with genetic engineering, an industry now more than two decades old. Once viewed as curious for its ability to make tomatoes turn red or to grow strawberries in the dead of winter, genetic engineering has advanced to the point where scientists can patent and sell new forms of life. Whether designing new animal breeds or altering the DNA composition of existing life, genetic engineers have created a new world with staggering implications for life as we know it. While biotechnology experts tout their findings as the keys to ending disease and lengthening life, critics have expressed concerns regarding irresponsibility, uncontrolled profits, and industry anarchy.[17] The implications of these changes are almost incalculable, and the media have raised the issues appropriately. Yet, other than esoteric professional science organization meetings at locations off the beaten path, this phenomenon has generated little reaction either from the public or from public policy makers.

A recent study shows, in fact, that the media are far from complete in their effort to capture public attention. As Shanto Iyenger and Donald Kinder point out in their examination of the role of media in American politics, "people do not pay attention to everything. To do so would breed paralysis."[18] In fact, particularly in this era of "information overload," people are quite selective about what they want to know. Compelling issues may not garner public attention because of their timing, difficulty, manner of presentation, or intrinsic interest. Nevertheless, if the triggering mechanism is serious, if enough people are sensitive to the issue, and if the event receives sufficient media exposure, chances are that a once-private matter will find its way to the public agenda.

Interest Groups

In postindustrial society, the line between private power and public policy is so faint that the components of politics almost appear as one. Volumes of literature have addressed the effects of private interests on public decisions. Some scholars have suggested that organized interests play necessary and even pivotal roles in establishing the public agenda. In her work *Group Power*, Carol Greenwald argues that "groups act mainly as information conduits for the formulation and advocacy of policy ideas."[19] But, counters Jeffrey Berry, the relationship between organized interests and government is much more a two-way street than many believe. Particularly with business interests, Berry notes, public policy makers "feel responsible for keeping the corporate sector satisfied with the state of the business climate. Government even takes responsibility for helping key industries or companies that are in trouble," as exemplified by favorable "bailout" legislation for Lockheed; for Chrysler; and, more recently, for the entire savings and loan industry.[20]

That interest groups place issues on the public agenda seems to be indisputable. What remains disputable is the extent to which their private objectives are compatible with public needs. Such is precisely the concern of Theodore Lowi, who laments that interest groups define the agenda on their terms, leaving to government the task of ratifying such private determinations through "public" policy commitments.[21] Yet, other examinations suggest that interest groups are not particularly unified, and therefore are not very successful in organizing the public agenda. Thus, in his study of interest group efforts to gain policy advantages, William Browne concludes, "there exists no particularly good reason to believe that organized groups are indeed real and cohesive interests rather than organizations of individuals with potentially conflicting views."[22]

Although the desirability of group representation in the official decision making process arena remains a question of debate, it is clear that groups do have a role in setting portions of the public agenda. One notable example is the close association between farmers and government. Viewed historically as the last bastion of rugged individualism, farmers have enjoyed a special role in building the public agenda through farm organizations. Programs developed by the Soil Conservation Service, the Corps of Engineers, and the Bureau of Reclamation have been designed in response to the demands of farmer and rancher constituents.[23] Popular thought holds that the American Farm Bureau Federation is most influential in setting the agricultural agenda when Republicans are in power, while the National Farmers Union has the most leverage during Democratic administrations.

Perhaps the most controversial of all agricultural issues has been the general question of farm subsidies, dollars paid to growers either for not producing their crops or as extra payment for producing their crops. Even though the necessity of government programs has been questioned, federal subsidies have nearly tripled from $9 billion to $25 billion during the decade between 1988 and 1997. Much of this increase has been due to the ability of farmers to make their issues public. Consider the matter of bee subsidies. Although three successive presidential administrations have sought to eliminate this program, beekeepers have offered a variety of reasons for retaining it. Among them: without subsidies, the bee industry would vanish, crops would not be pollinated properly, and foreign competitors would take over the U.S. honey market. One subsidy recipient argued that without bee subsidies, the government would no longer be able to keep African killer bees from overtaking their friendly bee counterparts in America![24] Together, these arguments have not only kept the bee subsidy issue on the public agenda, but have managed to keep policy makers from eliminating the funds.

Aside from agriculture, a multitude of other interests have helped to set the public agenda. Consider a few recent examples:

- The American Federation of Labor and Congress of Industrial Organizations (AFL-CIO) has attempted to discuss working conditions with respect to on-site picketing and strikebreaker employment.
- The American Medical Association (AMA), the Pharmaceutical Research and Manufacturers Association, the National Federation of Independent Businesses, and the Health Insurance Association of America, among many other interests, have dueled over control of the health reform issue.
- The American Legion has fought to protect veterans' benefits, as well as to influence military and defense matters.
- Both the National Organization of Women (NOW) and the Christian Coalition have taken stands on the abortion issue, each attempting to capture the attention of public policy makers for its own position.

These are but a few of the many groups that endeavor to mold the public agenda to reflect their values and needs.

Turf Wars

With so many actors attempting to define public policy issues, sometimes two or more may struggle over control of the "spin," or the official diagnosis. When such disputes occur, the wheels of agenda build-ing slow down because of conflicting signals on the agenda-building track. The shaping of the public policy issues surrounding the crash of Trans-World Airlines (TWA) flight 800 into the Atlantic in 1996 con-stitutes a case in point. For months after the tragedy, both the National Traffic Safety Board (NTSB) and the Federal Bureau of Investigation (FBI) examined the wreckage, with each agency prepared to set the agenda within its own framework. For the NTSB, the question cen-tered on safety; for the FBI, the issue focused on sabotage. Without sufficient evidence pointing in either direction, the two government agencies contested for control of the investigation, all the while main-taining a cooperative official posture before the cameras and the watchful public. As a result, neither theory was expressed with any enthusiasm, thereby leaving the entire issue in the backwater of the public agenda.

Coping with the Public Agenda

As discussed in chapter 1, virtually any issue can become the founda-tion for public policy. But resolution of troubling questions can take place only after such matters as pressing elements of the policy process have met the test. Even then, some issues on the public agenda are relatively immediate and concrete, while others are poorly defined and almost abstract .

After a triggering mechanism (or a series of triggering mechanisms) has converted an event into a public policy issue, the new agenda item awaits disposition by decision-making authorities. Yet, just as issues are born out of unique circumstances and promoted by various combi-nations of agents, they are likewise resolved in different fashions. Here we are reminded of scope, intensity, and timing, the critical elements of triggering mechanisms. The more that an issue embodies these properties, the more likely it is that the issue will receive serious atten-tion and response by policy makers. If either scope or intensity remains without audiences or reactions, and if such conditions do not deepen over time, it is not as likely that policy makers will react to the issue in a thorough, deliberative fashion.

Needless to say, some subjectivity creeps into the classification of policy issues as components of the public agenda, especially to the extent that they are complex or that they affect different sectors of society unevenly. Subjectivity aside, certain kinds of issues seem to generate far more comprehensive attention and replies than others. For our purposes, we may divide the issues awaiting resolution into two types: the substantive agenda and the symbolic agenda.

The Substantive Agenda

Substantive agenda management incorporates the most far-reaching and potentially explosive issues of public policy. So critical and divisive are the issues on the substantive policy agenda that they usually spark serious debate and precipitate great conflict among the public and among public policy makers.

Three elements are necessary for a policy question to be on the substantive agenda. First, the allocation of considerable public resources must be at stake. Second, the issue must generate massive amounts of attention from the citizenry and from public policy makers alike. Third, the issue must contain the potential for great change. Substantive questions are sufficiently broad in scope and of such high intensity that public debates can occur at length and, occasionally, at a feverish pitch. More important, their urgency demands response from those in position to make change.

Commonly, though not always, *economic issues* provide a number of substantive questions for the public agenda. Few economic issues affect people as directly and broadly as tax policy. Governments not only use taxes to extract more from some people and less from others, but they also use these monies to fund programs that have uneven impacts. As George Edwards and Ira Sharkansky point out, whether a policy issue centers on energy, employment, or education, "a great deal more political conflict occurs over the question of who pays and who benefits from a policy, than over the adoption or scope of the policy."[25]

When the government exercises its authority to extract taxes, its policy makers determine how these monies will be allocated. And when policy makers decide to change the rules under which taxes are collected by taxing some people more or others less, they raise questions not only on the tax policy question per se, but also on the merits of the myriad programs and groups that benefit from those monies. Under such conditions, the presentation of one issue may be the spawning grounds for many others.

In recent years, economic questions have been joined by other pressing issues that are debated by policy makers. Inasmuch as the policies of the New Deal and the Great Society eras established income floors for most Americans, increasing public attention has focused on noneconomic issues like immigration, racial integration, the environment, capital punishment, violence, drugs, and abortion. Clearly, *social questions* like abortion, school prayer, and gun control now loom as vital elements of the substantive public policy agenda. Nevertheless, given the powerful antitax sentiment and increasing concerns with annual unbalanced budgets, one wonders whether public policy makers will address substantive social issues with the vigor used for economic questions such as trade policy or minimum income patterns.[26]

The answer may come with new public policy commitments that simultaneously address social and economic issues as a single intertwined theme. For example, the sweeping reform of immigration law enacted by Congress in 1996 was touted by proponents as making both social and economic policy. The new law denies opportunities to illegal (and, in some cases, legal) immigrants, while providing fewer government dollars in the form of welfare, health care, and other areas of programmatic assistance.

The Symbolic Agenda

In addition to the substantive questions that dominate the public agenda, symbolic issues also share the political spotlight. These questions focus more on values than on resources. While large expenditures or transfers of power are not at stake with symbolic issues, nevertheless they may capture the attention of the public and of decision makers alike. The concept of good citizenship, for example, is symbolic because it centers on the "rights" and "wrongs" of society.

Much of the fuss about flag burning during the Bush administration coalesced not around public disturbances, but around patriotism. Recently, the issue of child abuse has attracted the attention of the public because of the sense of indecency that is connected with harm to an innocent child who has no defense against the physical strength of adults or older children. In each of these instances, the primary issue centers on values more than the distribution of authority or resources. Symbolic issues, therefore, tug at our collective consciences.

Symbolism is an important element of politics everywhere. Rites of passage such as scout badge awards or the celebration of long-term employment draw on symbolism. Not only do these activities speak of character, but they also spill over into political expectations. Hannah Pitkin writes that "when we speak of something as symbolizing . . . we are emphasizing the symbol's power to evoke feelings or attitudes. And we are calling to attention a vagueness, looseness, and partial quality of the reference."[27] The ambiguity of symbolism gives the concept an important role in the organization of the public agenda.

Symbolism is also important for its ability to transform relatively narrow themes or actions into broad issues. Such uses—and abuses—can quickly impact the public agenda. President Clinton reproached paramilitary political extremists who were thought to be responsible for the bombing of the Federal Building in Oklahoma for using "our sacred symbols (liberty) for paranoid purposes." Referring to the vigilante attitudes of militants, the president asked, "How dare you call yourselves patriots and heroes? . . . [T]here is no right to resort to violence when you don't get your way."[28] Clinton also exhibited his own symbolism by making a major policy address on terrorism in Michigan, thought to be the home of those responsible for the terrorist attack on the Oklahoma Federal Building.

Substantive Issues, Symbolic Responses. Symbolic policies are adopted by government decision makers for several reasons. There are times, for example, when narrowly based groups demand attention from government leaders with respect to a concern that is not widely shared throughout society. In other words, while the intensity among those affected may be considerable, the scope is likely to be quite narrow. Under these conditions, public policy makers may reply with a token or symbolic response that acknowledges the importance of the issue but that, simultaneously, does little to solve the problem.

The issue of government waste serves as a case in point. In January 1993, the Government Accounting Office (GAO) reported fraudulent and wasteful government in budget areas ranging from defense to Medicare,[29] a theme vigorously argued by Bill Clinton in his 1992 quest for the presidency. Immediately after taking office, President Clinton responded to the waste claim by asking Vice-President Al Gore to head a prestigious committee that would conduct a "national performance review" of virtually every federal program. Nine months later, the vice-president submitted a 168-page report with 800 recommendations for savings of $108 billion over five years. Given projected federal budgets totaling $8 trillion over the same period, the proposals amounted to a savings of 1.35 percent, nearly 40 percent of which would come from slashing the federal workforce, not programs.[30] In fact, despite close scrutiny and much criticism of the federal budget, few changes other than a 10 percent reduction of the federal workforce actually occurred, but the issue nonetheless was the subject of much public fanfare.

On other occasions, public agenda issues may be so multifaceted in nature that policy makers may be unable to resolve them in meaningful ways because of political, economic, or powerful group pressures. At such moments, policy makers find themselves in a bind: on the one hand, the demands for change are great; on the other hand, despite the cry that *something* should be done, there is virtually no consensus over *what* should be done. This contradiction surrounds the issue of health reform.

From patients to providers, virtually everyone has clamored for health care reform. In 1990, a nationwide poll found Americans believing by a 2 to 1 majority that the nation's health care system was in need of fundamental overhaul.[31] Not only did this dissatisfaction become an issue in the 1992 presidential contest, but President Bill Clinton made it a centerpiece of his reform efforts in 1993. By the end of the year, the president proposed an ambitious plan with universal medical coverage, new costs for employers, new taxes to make up the financing shortfall, and strict controls on insurance companies.[32] The possibility of dramatic change sparked resistance from several quarters, including insurance companies, medical organizations, and business alliances. The bill stalled. By 1995, a new Republican majority in Congress reframed the health care debate, focusing it on proposed cutbacks in Medicare, a program for the nation's seniors.[33] Now it was President Clinton's turn to be on the defensive. In the end, the substantive issue of health care reform was addressed by the Health Care Portability and Accountability Act of 1996, a largely symbolic law that permits workers to take health insurance programs with them when they leave their places of employment.

Aside from domestic concerns, substantive issues in the international arena often receive symbolic attention. Nowhere is this more delicate than with the issue of human rights. To date, the U.S. government's response to human rights violations has been minimal, partially because of the disagreement over the meaning of the term, partially because some U.S. companies doing business in contested nations would suffer more than others, and partially because many of the nations with undesirable conditions are U.S. allies. Thus, proclamations of symbolic quality occasionally have been uttered as expressions of U.S. views, although the real issues remain unresolved. Likewise, there are times when the United States can do little more than offer symbolic attention to substantive issues elsewhere because the consequences of U.S. intervention would be far more serious than any criticism of passive or removed behavior. Such has been the case in venues like the Middle East, where hostilities are so high and distrust so profound that any U.S. involvement other than "handholding" could very well tilt American public opinion in unpredictable directions as well as draw the wrath of nations around the world.

Complicated policy problems discourage comprehensive changes or policy commitments. In the words of one political analyst, "the greater the number of issue arenas a given policy cuts across, the more comprehensive the policy is. As such, it presents a highly complex set of choices to clientele and also confronts the analyst with numerous problems."[34] In these cases, symbolic attention may be given to substantive issue areas because minimum response is the only feasible response.

The "safety-valve" nature of symbolic public policy allows the agenda to seemingly include the perception of many more changes than actually take place. Stated in other words, symbolic public policies offer the illusion of redress. Robert Eyestone explains this phenomenon by stressing that "symbolic responses are effective in producing quiescence among target groups. Symbolic reassurance *is* satisfying, especially if there is no realistic prospect of anything concrete."[35] Thus, symbolic acknowledgment of a problem can simultaneously soothe alienated elements of society and produce minimal change.

The Hidden Agenda Allegation

Thus far, our discussion has centered on agenda builders and methods of categorizing the issues deliberated by public policy makers. While such considerations are vital to the public policy process, we do not mean to imply that all issues are decided automatically at appropriate policy making junctions. Whether they are substantive or symbolic, issues gain access to the public agenda only after fulfilling certain basic requirements. Roger Cobb and his associates suggest that three criteria must be met before an issue can be considered by policy makers: (1) the specific issue must be the subject of widespread attention; (2) a sizable proportion of the public must demand action; (3) the issue must be the concern of an appropriate governmental unit.[36] These three ingredients apply to a wide variety of circumstances and are necessary preconditions to the policy making process.

The implied assumption here is that the agenda-building process is open, at least in a democracy such as the United States. Accordingly, in such an environment, virtually all issues, symbolic or substantive, will appear and will be available for resolution, if they trigger sufficient scope and intensity within the appropriate time frame. Of course, agenda building depends upon the ability of agents to increase awareness of triggering mechanisms. Should this connection not be made, chances are good that a consensus for change will not develop.

But is the political system open to change? Is there sufficient linkage between those *with* an agenda and those who have the ability to resolve issues *on* the agenda? A large body of literature confirms that the public is generally comfortable with the political system, the decision-making process, and the distribution of public policies.[37] Nevertheless, there are those who argue that a *hidden agenda* has been suppressed by key leaders in government and society. This agenda contains some of the most potentially provocative questions for public policy authorities, yet they are rarely addressed.

More times than not, debates about hidden issues take place along esoteric lines of academic discourse.[38] However, sometimes alienation lurking just beneath the surface of ho-hum, everyday politics rears its head in an unpredictable, violent manner. Adherents of these values— thought to be few in number—reject the legitimacy of U.S. government because they believe that public policy makers are conspiring with other nations or minority groups to keep basic freedoms from everyone else.[39] Perhaps the darkest side of the bombing of the Federal Building in Oklahoma City in 1995 emerged with the claim by Federal Bureau of Investigation authorities that political extremists were responsible for the explosion.[40] Another example centers on the long-held claim that the assassination of President John Kennedy in 1963 was a secret communist plot covered over by official policy making authorities.[41]

Inasmuch as agenda building is a critical forerunner to decision making, it is important to know not only whether certain subjects might be excluded from debate, but why. The agenda-building criteria set forth by Cobb and his colleagues earlier in this chapter also shed considerable light on how issues are excluded from public discourse. Clearly, for questions to remain off the public docket, the issues must (1) receive little attention from the general public, (2) be understood by few or, if comprehended, be advocated by relatively powerless sectors of society, and (3) fall outside the jurisdiction of any government unit. Of course, it may be difficult to distinguish between relatively inconsequential matters, which naturally fail to capture sufficient scope and intensity, and vital issues that are intentionally suppressed because of their potential scope and intensity. As long as such ambiguity exists, some alienated elements of society will, in all likelihood, advocate the hidden-agenda framework.

The hidden-agenda concept is an important ingredient in the study of public policy because of its potential impact on the political process. The degree to which people believe in the existence of a hidden agenda may have a proportionally negative effect on the legitimacy of public institutions and actors. If decisions made outside government are widely interpreted as circumventing or neutralizing the actions of government, then the public policy making machinery loses substantial credibility.

Those who argue the existence of a hidden agenda usually make their claim on the basis that power flows outside of—and around—government. Under these circumstances, major policies are orchestrated or prevented by powerful private interests in order to minimize the redistribution of resources or political clout. Such intentional, persistent activities keep a select few in their influential positions, enabling them to design the agenda as they wish.[42]

That policy makers simply decide not to act on a question does not necessarily support the existence of a hidden agenda. It is only if public authorities contrive to ignore an issue or if they are somehow prevented from addressing an issue that such inaction would provide the framework of a hidden agenda. In other words, conspiracy is a vital element of this point of view, and hidden-agenda proponents believe that such behavior is common by those connected with the public policy process.[43] What makes all of this so intriguing is the lack of systematic proof necessary to determine the existence of the non-observable. Nevertheless, there is enough anecdotal evidence to feed the appetites of those who view politics as a closed process. The investigative outcome of the financial industries scandal of the late 1980s represents a case in point, not only because of the way that the issue seemed to hold policy makers hostage, but also because it appeared, to some, that the infested industry was regulated by former industry participants.[44] Conclusion: the "system" is closed, and the topics are restricted to the few who rule.

Conspiracy implies the collaboration of a small group of power brokers who are able to carefully control what appears on the public agenda. Yet, with so many information sources, it is difficult to keep news and/or crises from appearing in public view. Moreover, the fragmented nature of the American political system may make it difficult for privately orchestrated policies to emerge. As Clifton McCleskey notes, "the breadth of the interpersonal network necessary for power helps to ensure that it cannot be exercised in absolute or capricious fashion; there are too many opportunities for those with opposing viewpoints to withhold assistance in implementation, to mobilize counterpower, to appeal to lateral or higher authorities."[45]

The discussion of policy manipulation by few has generated considerable debate in American politics. When the bulk of society has seemed relatively content, the hidden-agenda argument has attracted few supporters. During times of political unrest, economic instability, or alienation, the hidden agenda theory is revived throughout the political spectrum. Given the political and economic uncertainties of the 1990s, we turn to a closer investigation of the hidden agenda and its effects on the public policy process.

The Hidden Agenda: Myth or Reality?

Perhaps the single most important staple of the hidden-agenda concept is the allegation that vital political questions are excluded from the public policy process by those who privately control such matters. We need, then, to determine the degree to which the public agenda is represented by public or private interests. E.E. Schattschneider addresses this question in his discussion of the power struggles within a conflict-laden society: "All forms of political organization have a bias in favor of the exploitation of some kinds of conflict and the suppression of others because organization is the mobilization of bias. Some issues are organized into politics while others are organized out."[46]

Simply stated, Schattschneider's view is that some will have the power to control events and policies, while others will not.

Peter Bachrach and Morton Baratz take the question of diminished public power one step closer to the hidden-agenda theme in their criticism of the public decision-making approach advocated by Robert Dahl.[47] Although they refer to political influence, their words also apply to the effectiveness of private controls over matters of public interest. Thus, Bachrach and Baratz write, "to measure relative influence solely in terms of the ability of public policy makers to initiate and veto proposals [through official government channels], is to ignore the possible exercise of influence or power in limiting the scope of initiation."[48] With respect to the two previous claims, we are still compelled to ask, is such control the result of arbitrary and capricious cunning or force, or is it due to varying amounts of interest and commitment?

The hidden-agenda argument is important not only because it potentially limits what comes out of government, but also because of the threat to the public good by the private few. If valid, this is a major flaw in the ability of public policy makers to address the pressing issues of the day. In fact, the extent to which the hidden-agenda claim is true could be considered an indictment of representative democracy. After all, how can the policies of a political system reflect public responses to public issues when the claims made upon that system are one-sided or misrepresented?

The hidden-agenda claim has never been quantified or proved, despite hypothetical and personal disappointments in the outcomes of various political activities. It is therefore difficult to separate myth from reality. Nevertheless, the fear of manipulation appeals to students of power theories as well as to those concerned with ensuring that public problems placed on the public agenda are truly representative.

Perhaps there is an explanation for the disparity between public and private goals. There is some evidence to suggest that political leaders and the public at large do not perceive issues in the same light or with a similar degree of concern. The participation study conducted by Sidney Verba and Norman Nie, for example, shows that leaders and followers do not necessarily view issues (or nonissues) from similar perspectives. At the same time, their conclusions hardly support the claim that the public agenda is privatized and twisted out of an intentional effort to deny the public its due: "It may not be that the *preferences* of the inactive on the issues of the day are replaced by the *preferences* of those who are active if political leaders pay attention to the activist population. It may be, rather, that the issues of the day are selected in a way that ignores whatever matters most to the inarticulate members of the population."[49] Similarly, Steven Rosenstone and John Mark Hansen explain the unevenness between leaders and followers in terms of resources rather than power: With values formed by education, wealth, and social networks, they note, "people with more abundant resources participate more in governmental politics than people with less abundant resources."[50] Carried to a logical conclusion, these studies imply that the public policy making process is governed less by sinister objectives than by different sets of perceptions between policy makers and the public and, additionally, within the public.

The Constellation of Issues—Too Big, Too Small, or Just Right?

The combination of substantive and symbolic issues that come and go, the existence of champions who are willing to promote them, and the political actors needed to turn ideas into policy are all necessary to create a public policy. Even with these prerequisites, policy decisions do not come out of thin air; rather, they emerge as the result of the information and pressures that have been placed upon policy makers. As John Kingdon summarizes, the sequence and outcomes are anything but automatic: "Through the imposition of criteria by which some ideas are selected out for survival while others are discarded, order is developed from chaos, pattern from randomness. . . . Proposals that are judged infeasible—that do not square with policy community values, that would cost more than the budget would allow, that run afoul of opposition in either the mass or specialized publics, or that would not find a receptive audience among elected politicians—are less likely to survive than proposals that meet these standards."[51] Conversely, should political leaders sense the broad scope and intense conflict surrounding an issue over a time span during which pressure grows, then in all likelihood they will use the powers of their offices to examine the issue in a wider context such as a public forum. Such are the realities of agenda building.

Some observers suggest that the public agenda has become hopelessly complex. As various factions define problems and approach government for solutions, the public agenda becomes so crowded that it results in political impotence. David Robertson and Dennis Judd refer to this as a "capacity" issue and note that the overloading of policy makers with too many issues can yield results ranging from incoherence to gridlock.[52] The resulting public agenda map may therefore leave decision makers at all levels of government frustrated in attempting to follow it, while the public grows ever more weary of inaction.

Considerable debate continues as to the advisability of an extensive public agenda, with its complement of fractured decision-making institutions and authorities. One recent study argues that an expanded public agenda not only signifies representation for several publics, but offers the opportunity for more resolution. Particularly with unpopular questions, Donald Baumer and Carl Van Horn write, "the struggle for establishing the policy agenda may be more important than the policy-making process because fundamental issues and alternatives are often defined at the selection stage."[53] The presentation of such issues, in turn, leads to wider debate because of the incorporation of ever-widening numbers of groups into the policy making process.

Others are quick to point out that an expanded agenda does not automatically result in the adoption of policies designed to promote the public good. Thus, Norman Ornstein and Shirley Elder suggest that with the proliferation of issues, the number of participants also grows. With this escalation, "groups become narrower and more specialized in their interests, and they deal with narrower and more specialized policy units."[54] The result is a larger bottleneck in the decision-making process, with an agenda overwhelming to public policy makers and frustrating to most segments of society except those who are able to generate results through skillful manipulation of the process.

Agenda Building—A Precondition for Policy Response

The proliferation of items on the public agenda has led to questions about the substantive and symbolic issues from which policies are made. Some scholars assert that "only a small fraction of all *potential* issues ever gets debated" because stable democracies can cope with only so many substantive questions at a time.[55] Dissenting observers are not as kind in their assessments of a limited public agenda. Instead, they argue, it is the intention of those in power to relegate substantive matters to the realm of things that get only symbolic responses. As Michael Parenti writes, "Although the decisions of government are made in the name of the entire society, they rarely benefit everyone. . . . [T]he existing political system responds primarily—although not exclusively—to the powers and needs of the corporate system."[56]

Given the pressures that accompany attempts to resolve substantive questions, symbolic policies are important to the public agenda. Since the public needs to feel that the political process works, the regular resolution of *something* from government is likely to be far more desirable than the repeated disappointments of stalemate.

It is not enough to explain public policy by looking at the decisions that emerge from government. Without an understanding of agenda development as well as the combination of issues available for resolution, policy analysis is a one-dimensional experience. Policy makers may be valuable catalysts for converting issues into commitments, but the public agenda constitutes the list from which they take their cues for action.

Questions for Further Thought

1. What is the relationship between triggering mechanisms and the public agenda?

2. Several actors are responsible for development of the public agenda. Who are they and what are their characteristics?

3. How do we differentiate between the substantive and the symbolic agendas? Are the distinctions important with respect to policy development?

4. Analyze the "hidden-agenda" theory. What evidence exists for supporting or refuting this claim?

Suggested Reading

Cigler, Allan J., and Burdette Loomis, *Interest Group Politics*, 4th ed. (Washington, DC: CQ Press, 1995).

Kingdon, John W., *Agendas, Alternatives, and Public Policies* (Boston: Little, Brown, 1984).

Lowi, Theodore J., *The End of Liberalism*, 2d ed., (New York: W.W. Norton, 1979).

Parenti, Michael, *Land of Idols* (New York: St. Martin's Press, 1994).

Robertson, David B., and Dennis R. Judd, *The Development of American Public Policy* (Glenview, IL: Scott, Foresman,1989).

Sherman, Arnold K., and Aliza Kolker, *The Social Bases of Politics* (Belmont, CA: Wadsworth, 1987).

Truman, David, *The Governmental Process* (New York: Alfred A. Knopf, 1951).

4 THE POLICY MAKERS: ROLES AND REALITIES

Up to this point, we have traced the public policy process as a series of events that build toward confusion, crisis, and change. The activities that lead up to policies are almost cacophonous in nature—some dramatic, others insignificant; some random, others patterned; some horrific, others humorous. What they have in common is a negative impact on the ebb and flow of everyday life for a sizable segment of the population. When adverse conditions and unexpected problems develop, we struggle to adapt to the circumstances and try to rearrange matters for the better.

The policy making process, we have noted, begins with triggering mechanisms, unexpected occurrences that disturb our routine environment. The more people who are affected in a similar manner, the more likely they will express their concerns to those who can do something about an unpleasant or harmful situation. But who receives and responds to these messages? In what arenas are solutions developed? And under what circumstances can we expect that those capable of effecting change will actually carry out such tasks? We find these answers by identifying and examining the roles of public policy makers, the actors in various levels of government who have the authority to convert prominent questions on the public agenda into appropriate policy commitments.

Particularly in a democracy, policy makers are in pivotal positions of power. These individuals must deal with a variety of competing interests and pressures so that, in the end, an improved condition results from their efforts. Their task is particularly difficult in a society such as the United States, where conflict is open and opinions are publicly expressed. Sometimes, the "improved" situation, or new policy, generates more flak than the condition that led to change; when that occurs, policy makers scurry back to an earlier position, or at least a place in the policy making process that gives them a greater sense of security. But what is most important to remember is that the policy maker is in the business of effecting change.

The value of the policy maker is analogous to the role of high temperature as a catalyst for converting water into steam energy. Without sufficient heat, water has limited use as a power source. With the proper amount of heat, water is converted to steam and, as a result, becomes an energy source with greatly improved utility. And so it is with policy makers. Without their action, problems flow without direction or the possibility of settlement. But when engaged in the process of resolution, the policy maker supplies the heat for government decisions.

Far more than simply an advocate of change, the policy maker has the obligation to alter society's political, social, and economic courses. So important is the policy maker's function in the political process that Charles Jones refers to this authority as "legitimation," an activity that establishes widely recognized ground rules for decision making and the specific means through which such actions can take place.[1] If the policy maker fails to heed the cries calling for change, he or she may become part of the large group stating needs instead of the select few who resolve them.

To be sure, not all agree that the *real* policy makers are found in the marble halls of government, where they eagerly wait to analyze and cope with every important public problem. As discussed toward the end of chapter 3, some observers caution that the most important issues are suppressed from the public agenda, that private interests—powerful in their own right—go outside of government for solutions to their concerns.

Suspicions about shady dealings notwithstanding, we do know that every year a huge national budget is passed, along with similar measures in state and local government jurisdictions. These documents are accompanied by thousands of laws defining how governments will collect and spend monies. We also know that, on a regular basis, government authorities decide outcomes about what is good for us, what is dangerous to us, and what is harmed by us. Decisions like these are reached regularly (if not easily) at all levels of society, from national to local, where units of people require rules and governance.

All of which takes us back to the concern of this chapter—a description of policy making actors, of their responsibilities, and of the rules under which they operate. And just who—or what—are these entities? The expanse of the answer to this question has grown with the evolution of society and modern government. Not so many years ago, the relevant actors were described as an intertwined *iron triangle* consisting of the bureaucracy, interest groups, and legislative committees.[2] In recent years, scholars have described key participants as members of *policy networks*, collections of individuals inside as well as outside the official boundaries of government.[3] Whether narrow or broad, the key point in describing policy makers is that such individuals are in the position of getting something done in an authoritative manner.

In assessing the relationship between politics and policies, Robert Lineberry writes that "at the core of the political system are the institutions and personnel of decision making."[4] For our purposes, policy makers are the personnel who, as the core of the political system, continually make it work by virtue of their commitments, their objectives, and their response patterns. While they are not necessarily responsible for formulating issues or even placing them on the public agenda, "the buck stops" at the policy makers' doors; they are accountable for the ways in which they manage (or refuse to manage) the issues placed before them.

The irony of the relationship is that often the expectations of policy makers exceed their abilities to perform. Much of the problem is determined by the limitations of power as prescribed in our constitutional arrangements.[5] For example, the push and pull of the federal arrangement often places local or state issues in national government hands; conversely, local or state authorities sometimes respond to nationwide issues in dramatically different ways. The first scenario leaves national policy makers accused of demagoguery, while the second scenario promotes inequality. As David Robertson and Dennis Judd state, "[the] fragmentation of decision making authority that characterizes the American political system has, over the long run, become a vehicle for frustrating policy reforms."[6] As a result, political actors in authoritative capacities sometimes seem to shoot off the mark, if not blanks.

The remaining sections of this chapter describe and analyze major policy making authorities in American politics. It should be understood that, while our attention will center on actors at the national level of government, equivalent political leaders and institutions exist at other levels of policy making authority as well. With such information, we will be in a better position to comprehend the role of these power brokers who provide policy responses for agenda matters.

Congress

Few institutions in American life have the historical significance of the U.S. Congress. While the constitutional framers clashed over countless issues, including the ways in which members of Congress would be selected, they agreed on the necessity for an independent legislature with extensive policy making authority. Randall Ripley concludes as much in his review of the constitutional convention debates of 1787: "[T]he principle that there would be a powerful legislature was never jeopardized."[7] As if to underscore Congress's role as the premier policy making branch, Article I, Section 8, of the Constitution awarded a variety of specific powers to the national legislature, as well as the ability to "make all laws which shall be necessary and proper" to execute its enumerated powers. Accordingly, the functions of the modern Congress have expanded with and adapted to the needs of modern society, many of which were never imagined at the time of the Constitution's design.

More than 200 years have passed since the adoption of the U.S. Constitution in its basic form. While Congress remains a pillar of the policy making process, not all agree that the legislative branch carries the same primacy carries as it enjoyed in the earliest days of the republic. For many congressional observers, the demands of modern times—ranging from clamoring constituencies to a powerful executive branch—have proved the need for and wisdom of a strong Congress. As Edward Schneier and Bertram Gross argue, "whatever Congress's failings or strengths, its responsibilities and concerns have grown at a staggering rate. Whatever its slice of power in comparison to the other branches of the federal government, its share is taken from a much larger pie."[8] Likewise, whatever evolution has occurred in American society, the policy making preeminence of Congress remains central to the political process.

That Congress has the capability to evolve as a policy making entity was demonstrated with the election of a Republican majority in 1994 and the emergence of Newt Gingrich as Speaker of the House of Representatives. While most of the nation focused on the much-touted Republican "Contract with America," Gingrich and his allies made organizational changes in the House, the outcome of which rejuvenated the prominence of the House as well as the power of its Speaker.[9] Less dramatic changes occurred with the emergence of a Republican majority in the U.S. Senate. Nevertheless, the transformation resulting from the election results and rules changes yielded a national legislature with an enhanced capability and an increased desire to confront the executive branch and, thus, to play a larger role in the policy making process.

Other assessments of Congress place the legislative branch in the category of a "has-been" institution, a relic of the past that is now either unable or unwilling to deal with pressing issues of the day. Such accounts imply that the Gingrich-led reforms may be more temporary than permanent. Long-term, comprehensive examinations of the policy making arena, writes Theodore Lowi, demonstrate that as the functions of government have become more complicated and more demanding, Congress has chosen to delegate rather than legislate. Lowi traces this transformation to the New Deal era of the 1930s. In response to the national emergency brought on by the Great Depression, an overwhelmed Congress began adopting general policy objectives instead of specific policy commitments. While Congress retained its reputation as the country's "chief legislature," it turned over the most important decisions to the president or to one of the many departments within the executive branch. Today, Lowi writes, the situation is much the same, whether the issue before Congress lies in the foreign or the domestic arena. The contemporary activities of Congress may be described as lawmaking, but in reality they are general policy orientations framed in ambiguous intent.[10] According to this viewpoint, Congress has lost much of its glitter as a proactive policy making authority, deferring instead to other institutions and actors.

A third interpretation of congressional behavior in the policy making process emphasizes the shift of power within Congress. Whereas scholars once focused on the "front-end power" associated with traditional committees,[11] reassessments of the legislative branch have turned increasingly to the power at the end of the congressional policy making cycle. Stephen Van Beek, for one, notes that the fragmentation of Congress resulting from post-Watergate reforms has led to the reliance upon *postpassage politics*, the politics of policy resolution that takes place in conference committees after the observable legislative ritual.[12] As such, the prowess of Congress has merely shifted to a less visible part of the institution.

These three positions underscore the controversy that surrounds the policy making capabilities of Congress in the 1990s—and, as often is the case in evaluating different points of view, each is partially correct. It is clear that Congress maintains its independence as a policy making authority.

On a few occasions, Congress has been so brazen as to enact public policy over the veto of a president. Such actions are rare, and they usually require a bipartisan spirit of cooperation, as was demonstrated with passage of the Civil Rights Restoration Act of 1988, a law that strengthened sanctions against gender and race discrimination, during the Reagan administration. President Clinton suffered a similar defeat in 1995, when Congress enacted the Private Securities Litigation Reform Act; the legislation protected corporations while limiting the rights of stockholders to engage in what some have called "frivolous" lawsuits.

Nowhere has the autonomy of the legislative branch been more evident in recent times than with the policies of the 104th Congress. Many of its most ambitious undertakings were grouped together as the Republican Contract with America, a comprehensive effort to drastically scale back national government responsibilities in the areas of budgeting, taxation, and policy reach, while returning critical functions to lower levels of government and eliminating many others altogether. In some instances, Democratic President Bill Clinton signed Republican policy initiatives such as welfare reform and stronger punishments for several categories of crimes, but in the more controversial areas dealing with social program reductions in the name of budget reform, Clinton used the veto to thwart the Republican effort. Even in its losses, however, the 104th Congress demonstrated an uncanny resolve, to the point of shutting down the federal government on two occasions during the struggle over the fiscal year 1997 federal government budget. Yet, the "bottom line" of the Gingrich-led assault, an independent account concluded, was "less a revolution than a conservative correction."[13]

Nevertheless, Congress continues to act without conviction or focus in many policy areas, often by assigning key activities to committee staff members or by permitting administrators to carry out functions that were once clearly under legislative control. For example, when defense downsizing became a way of life during the late 1980s and the early 1990s, key congressional staffers protected otherwise vulnerable programs under the jurisdiction of the National Aeronautics and Space

Administration (NASA), thereby reorganizing defense priorities in the process.[14] Likewise, when Congress enacted an education reform bill in 1990, sponsors relied heavily upon staff members to frame not only the issue but the need for legislation.[15]

Although Congress retains the ability to act independently, its behavior has become more unpredictable than in the past. A number of structural and political changes account for the new fluidity. First, today's Congress is a much more democratic, decentralized institution than in the past. Seniority used to be the congressional prerequisite for influence; now, committee chairpersons are chosen through elections of the party caucus. Also, whereas party leaders could once be assured of cooperation through the use of threats and rewards, many of their powers have been stripped away by congressional reforms, leaving rank-and-file members with an increased sense of independence.[16] Three recent ethics cases dealing with powerful members of Congress, Democratic Representative Dan Rostenkowski, Republican U.S. Senator Bob Packwood, and House Speaker Newt Gingrich, serve as vivid examples of Congress as an institution in which no one is beyond condemnation and punishment.[17]

The end-product of these changes has been the development of not one but several methods of operation by Congress in the policy making process. Therefore, the evaluation of its performance often depends upon many variables, including the types of issues at stake, affected populations, partisan differences, and power relationships. As David Vogler concludes, "some of the bills will be considered routine legislation, and others major policy proposals. Some will be perceived as having no direct effect on a particular legislator's constituents, whereas others will be seen as having a profound impact on the life-style or economic situation of every person in the state or district. All legislators, in short, develop some scheme for classifying policies.... Students of the congressional process must do the same thing."[18] Placed in perspective, Congress has the potential to play a large role in the public policy making process. The extent of its activity, however, is likely to depend upon the issue awaiting resolution.

President

If present-day evaluations of Congress as a policy making authority conflict, considerably more agreement prevails over the powers of the modern presidency. For better or worse, this institution has evolved as a formidable element in the policy making arena. With its high-profile emergence, the presidency has become the centerpiece of the nation's policy making network.

Until the Great Depression, the preponderance of presidential activities centered largely on administrative and facilitative functions. Only the most severe economic calamities or war-related conditions served as reasons for presidents to assume policy making stances—and then only on a temporary basis.[19] But modern presidents not only propose policies; they often make them and order their implementation by other agencies within the executive branch—sometimes with no endorsements other than their own sense of what should be done.

Although the early functions of Congress were defined by the Constitution in lengthy detail, the roles intended for the president initially were tentative and unclear. Fresh from their liberation in the struggle with the king of England, the leaders of the revolution were unwilling to create another monarch to serve as the nation's highest authority. At the same time, they understood that a fledgling nation required discipline, order, and, above all, leadership. This ambivalence carried over into constitutional provisions regarding the presidency. As James W. Davis summarizes, the founding fathers intentionally avoided being too specific about presidential powers in order to quell any concerns about monarchy or unaccountable dictators. In fact, "they seemed to want a president of somewhat limited powers ... , a chief executive who would remain above parties and factions, enforce the laws Congress passed, negotiate with foreign governments, and help the states in times of civil disorder."[20] Given these ambiguous duties, early presidents tended to be conservative with their authority, compared to the wide berth they occupy today.

As the nation grew and matured, the president's functions also expanded. To be sure, some responsibilities of the office are much the same today as they were when the institution was first established. For example, the president remains singularly important as head of state. The commander-in-chief role has changed only with respect to the weapons available, the extent of the military's reach, and the immediacy with which the president may order the use of force. However, the office of the chief executive has grown in new directions, particularly with respect to issues that impact the domestic arena. As noted in chapter 2, the development of electronic media constitutes a technological breakthrough with vast ramifications. In nationally broadcast addresses, the president has become a builder of the public agenda, presenting ideas and problems directly to the public and to other public policy makers. New communications methods now even allow audiences to call in to press conferences and ask their own questions, and owners of personal computers can express opinions to and get information from the president via the Internet.

The president also has become a prominent actor in the policy making arena. While he always has had the power to thwart congressional policy objectives through the use of the veto, the president has emerged as an architect of change through his own proactive initiatives. To be sure, presidents must beware of overloading the policy agenda with too many issues and policy making responses, thereby creating resistance or political stalemate from other policy makers. This caution notwithstanding, George Edwards and Stephen Wayne conclude that presidents now operate with a power arsenal of policy weapons: "With a national perspective, a large staff structure, and the ability to focus public attention and mobilize public support, presidents have been placed in a position to propose policy and get it adopted."[21] With the Office of the Management and Budget, the Council of Economic Advisors, and a cadre of skilled experts directly under his control, the president can persuasively frame issues on his terms.

As a policy making actor, the president seems most powerful in times of deadlock and crisis. For example, President Ronald Reagan and Congress tangled over the budget in 1981, while the public waited to see who would blink first. In this case, the president threatened to veto appropriations bills that exceeded what he considered reasonable expenditure levels. Congress ignored the president's warning and passed a bill that went beyond Reagan's limit. In response, the president vetoed the bill. For more than twenty-four hours, the United States was technically bankrupt and out of business. Finding itself under pressure from a variety of sources, Congress buckled under to the president's policy viewpoint and quickly supplied a new budget within his guidelines.

Another example of presidential clout occurred in 1995 with the action by President Clinton to rescue the Mexican economy, when Mexico suddenly plunged to the brink of bankruptcy. With U.S. interests fundamentally intertwined with those of Mexico, Clinton asked Congress to approve a $40 billion loan package. Leaders in the legislative branch balked at the president's "fast-track" demand, and set out to schedule lengthy hearings. Feeling the need to move quickly, Clinton committed $20 billion from a special U.S. Treasury fund usually intended for stabilizing the dollar. Although many members of Congress publicly criticized the president for unilateral behavior, many were privately relieved.[22] Clinton pointed to his Mexico bailout as evidence of his foreign policy skills in his 1996 reelection effort, reaping further gains from his earlier action.

The widely acknowledged ascendant power of the presidency has not met with universal acclaim. Ever protective of the separation-of-powers concept so important to American government, some critics commonly point to a shift in the constitutional balance, with the presidency usurping policy-formulating authority historically reserved for Congress. Citing his interpretation of the Constitution and its assignment of powers, historian Arthur Schlesinger wrote, more than a quarter century ago, "there is no evidence that . . . his office as Commander in Chief endowed the president with an independent source of authority," particularly as it applies to the domestic policy arena.[23]

Other observers believe that the presidency should be even more expansive as the linchpin of the nation's public policy making machinery. "Quite simply," Samuel Kernell writes, "the American public holds the president responsible for promoting the general welfare."[24] Certainly the end of the Cold War and emergence of the United States as the world's only superpower allow the president and the nation to focus on domestic issues in ways they never have done before in the nation's history.[25] Accordingly, the president can carry out such a broad mandate only if he is in the middle of the policy mix.

Debate notwithstanding, it is clear that the passive presidency of years past has given way to the activist institution of today. To this end, whether the officeholder's orientation is liberal, conservative, or anything in between, presidents can and do make a range of policy decisions through executive orders, the abolishment or creation of government agencies, and executive agreements with the heads of other nations. Conservative President Ronald Reagan did as much in 1981 when he unilaterally signed an executive order requiring all regulatory agencies to submit proposed rules to the Office of Management and Budget. Liberal President Bill Clinton did as much in 1994 when he committed U.S. troops to Haiti as part of an effort to usher out a dictatorship and to usher in a previously elected leader. On the domestic front, Clinton showed his willingness to assume sole responsibility for environmental policy making in 1996 when he signed an executive agreement making 1.7 million acres of land in Utah a national preserve. Such increased power not only makes the president a vital policy maker; it also points to the fundamental, if gradual, rearrangement of previous policy making structures and relationships.

Nevertheless, it is not yet clear whether the reality of the modern activist presidency truly matches the rhetoric surrounding the office and often promised by its occupant. Such doubts have surfaced over all recent presidencies, including that of Bill Clinton. David Stoesz argues that Clinton came to his presidency with the promise of major change in the areas of health, urban renewal, immigration, social security, and welfare. Stoesz adds, "Once inaugurated, however, the oft-evoked 'CHANGE' turned out to be small change, indeed."[26] Why did the administration fall short? Perhaps because the president did not have the tools (and the clout) to live up to his own expectations.

Against this uncertainty is the addition of the line-item veto to the arsenal of presidential weaponry. Passed by Congress and signed into law by President Clinton in 1996, the new law permits the president to cut individual items from spending bills, thereby eliminating wasteful "pork" without vetoing the entire bill. While the new law places the chief executive under more pressure, it will also give the president even more power to shape public policy.

Judiciary

Virtually every high school civics class and, regrettably, too many college-level government courses offer the following description of power at the national level: the president proposes policies and signs the laws that emerge from these and other initiatives, Congress assumes responsibility for turning ideas into public policies, and the courts restrict their activities to carefully measured interpretations of the law. The only problem with this traditional characterization of the separation of powers is that it is dead wrong. Whatever the historical merit of this description, it simply does not reflect the realities of contemporary American politics. While it is difficult to compare the influence of one institution with that of another, we know that the judiciary is far from passive. In fact, for some time now, the judiciary has been *active* in the policy making process, with its decisions often having as much impact as an executive order or a congressional statute. Indeed, in most cases, the "law of the land" simply is not such until—and unless—it garners judicial approval.

Such was not always the case with the role of the American courts. Particularly at the national level, the decisions of the Supreme Court appeared to fluctuate in response to changing national needs and priorities. Yet, along with the appearance of superficial vacillation, the judiciary developed a deep sense of itself and its own role in the policy making apparatus of American politics. As Mary Walker states, "In a sense, the Court interpreted its way into the leading role it was to play in the process—that of constitutional umpire. The Court assumed the power to invalidate acts of people in other components of the system when those acts were—in the Court's opinion—contrary to the Constitution."[27] That power became known as *judicial review*. Although the Constitution made no such allowances for the Court's behavior, many state courts had already moved in the direction of legislative review. Thus, when the U.S. Supreme Court moved in the same direction, its new behavior drew surprisingly little opposition. In the process, the stage was set for the judiciary's adoption of a major national policy making role.

The Court began its new policy making activity with caution. At first, most interpretations of statutes and the Constitution were responses to narrow economic questions. Until well into the twentieth century, the federal judiciary focused on policy issues related to property, capital and labor, interstate commerce, and other areas that dealt with the flow of goods. In most cases, the Court allowed the states rather than the national government to establish whatever regulations might be necessary.

As the twentieth century approached its midpoint, the Court changed in two important ways. Beginning in the 1930s, the federal judiciary reassessed the position of the national government via-à-vis the states. In more cases than not, the Court declared that the Constitution intended broader powers for the federal government than for the states and that, when the two levels clashed over policy authority, the federal government would prevail.[28]

The second change became evident in the 1950s, when the Court began to consider the constitutionality of policy decisions in issue areas outside the traditional economic sphere. Questions of economic discrimination, apportionment, welfare, abortion, civil liberties, and environmental protection gradually were brought into the Court's domain and accepted by the jurists as material for response within its expanding areas of authority. The more the judiciary considered the merits of broad social issues, the more the Court's role as a policy making agent became recognized.

The activist courts during the mid-twentieth century had decidedly liberal economic and social bents, but activism can move in conservative directions as well. Beginning with the tenure of Chief Justice Warren Burger (1969–85), the Court's activism swung in the direction of strong support for law enforcement and the prosecution in criminal cases. In the process, U.S. Supreme Court majorities overturned numerous state and lower federal court decisions—hardly an endorsement of the status quo. In areas other than criminal procedure, notes one student of the judiciary, the Burger Court "was no more deferential than its predecessor to Congress or to state regulatory efforts affecting Commerce,"[29] although the policy outcomes were in a radically different direction.

With the departure of Chief Justice Burger, the general conservative tone of the Court continued. By 1995, a narrow majority of the Court, now under the guidance of Chief Justice William Rehnquist, restricted the power of national government even more through a narrow interpretation of the interstate commerce clause, long thought to be the basis through which Congress could legislate on activities ranging from civil rights to working conditions. The end result was the rejection of a recent federal law banning firearms within 1,000 feet of public schools.[30]

Yet the Court has not been as conservative as some critics have suggested. For example, one month after the firearms case, the justices overturned state laws that provided term limits for elected federal offices. Writing for a narrow 5 to 4 majority, Justice Paul Stevens noted that "a state-imposed restriction is contrary to the fundamental principle of our representative democracy, embodied in the Constitution, that the people should choose who they please to govern them."[31]

What do we make from these decisions, one striking down a federal law and other striking down state laws? In each case, the Court struck out against policy making bodies that exceeded their spheres of authority. In the process, the Court has moved vigorously to assert its own authority. The question remains, has the Court gone too far?

Whether the Supreme Court has overstepped its authority in the policy making process is a question with varied answers. For example, Robert Dahl has written that every time the Court supplants public opinion or national law with its own policy, the Court threatens its own legitimacy.[32] To that Nathan Glazer adds, "there is the legitimate fear that disorder will prevail if the means by which complicated issues are settled [through the Court] in a complex society are themselves brought under attack."[33] The essence of this argument is that power has limits; it is neither absolute nor without checks. The Court jeopardizes its political health when it reverses too many policy commitments made by other institutions and actors. Decisions by the Warren Court on civil liberties and, more recently, decisions by the Rehnquist Court concerning flag burning and the presence of gays in the military demonstrate the extent to which the Court's policy pronouncements can generate public ire.

Other analysts place the role of the Court in a fairly harmless perspective. Henry Abraham notes that the judiciary's unpopular policies are not without sanctions. The Court may be reversed by legislation, by Constitutional amendment, and even by itself in future cases. In fact, he argues, "There is little doubt that, generally speaking, the policy of the Court—whose members, after all, are 'children of their times'—never departs drastically from the policy of the lawmaking majority in the long run."[34] Such behavior is hardly coincidental, notes Peter Woll, because as part of its effort to preserve independence, the Court is careful to exercise self-restraint in sensitive policy areas when its members sense that other branches may work to curb its powers.[35]

Although the propriety of the Court's policy making activity remains controversial, its emergence as a policy actor in modern government is beyond question. The Court's assumption of authority has also had profound repercussions on other policy making bodies, which must coexist with the judiciary in ways never fully anticipated. Furthermore, there is the question of judicial selection. Since a simple majority of the nine members can issue opinions that have sizable impacts, it is little wonder that nominations to fill vacancies on the bench stir up so much commotion.

Bureaucracy

Congress, the president, and the judiciary are the most recognized policy making actors in American society. Although they may differ in function and design, these institutions share the same historical bond: they are products of the Constitution and of subsequent interpretations of that document. The bureaucracy, however, is another matter. Here is a policy making structure—or a series of structures—that has evolved over time in its relationship to other policy making authorities and in its self-assumed ability to decide policy matters. Whatever independence the bureaucracy has, however, we must bear in mind that it is a creation of the traditional policy making institutions.

What does the term *bureaucracy* mean? For our purposes, bureaucracies are units of government that both make and implement public policies. They differ from the "mainline" institutions, discussed above, in the manners in which they are organized. Bureaucracies are established by other policy makers; in almost all instances, they are created by legislative mandates or executive orders. Because of their dependence upon other units of government for their existence, bureaucracies are vulnerable to change at almost any time.

There is a second way in which bureaucracies are different from other policy making authorities: for the most part, bureaucrats are civil servants. Whether they deliver mail, evaluate tax returns, or monitor the quality of agriculture commodities, bureaucrats are generally part of the civil service system. Other than a select few political appointees, they are hired by merit and, often, for their skill sets. Given their potential lengthy stay in the same line of work, bureaucrats often develop expertise that exceeds and outlasts that of other policy makers, most of whom have comparatively brief stays in elective or appointed political offices. Thus, bureaucrats offer the qualities of continuity and stability.

Bureaucracies come in different shapes and sizes, with varying amounts of policy making authority. Gathered under the jurisdictional umbrella of the executive branch are fourteen of the nation's largest bureaucracies, including the Department of Defense (DOD), with 969,000 civilian employees; the Department of Veterans Affairs, with 248,000; and the Department of the Treasury, with 158,000. At the other end are the relatively small Department of Housing and Urban Development (HUD), with 13,000; and the Department of Education, with 5,000. A number of other large bureaucracies outside the executive branch perform vital government functions. Among these are independent agencies, like the National Aeronautics and Space Administration (NASA), with 24,000 employees; government corporations such as the

Postal Service, with 777,000 employees; and regulatory commissions as typified by the Interstate Commerce Commission (ICC), with 625 employees.

The size of a bureaucracy often has no relationship to its ability to formulate and execute public policy. For example, despite congressional legislation placing a "procurement czar" in the Department of Defense, evidence shows that the DOD has been unable to develop sound procedures for dealing with waste and fraud.[36] Yet, for most of the 1990s, the Federal Communications Commission (FCC) and its 1,500-member staff have promulgated and implemented numerous— and often conflicting—policies regarding the regulation of the cable industry. The relatively small Food and Drug Administration (FDA), similarly, has issued rules on vitamin claims, putting a $4 billion industry on notice.[37]

Although bureaucracies were initially designed as policy executors— agencies organized to administer what authoritative sources created— their roles have expanded with the evolution of society. For more than a half century, observers have tracked bureaucratic expansion not only in terms of new responsibilities but also in terms of basic decision-making tasks. A good deal of the change in the United States has occurred since World War II, but even before that period, Carl J. Friedrich cautioned that the legislative experience was a far-from-complete description of the policy making process. He argued that to look at legislating alone was to ignore the presence of administrative officials who, by virtue of their managerial positions, were able to participate continuously and significantly in the policy process long after basic decisions were made.[38] Such proximity to the locus of power gave bureaucrats policy making authority.

Friedrich's early analysis injected unusual candor and insight into public administration. Nevertheless, some students of the subject rejected the concept of bureaucratic policy making authority. Instead, the counterargument held, bureaucracies were simply logical extensions of the political process. Wrote the authors of one study, bureaucracies "cannot exist without appropriations in enabling statutes. They can survive only as long as they can combine to secure . . . legislative and executive support."[39] In effect, then, this view classifies bureaucracies as recipients of command rather than authorizers of policy.

Today, the debate is not about whether the bureaucracy makes policy; rather, what is being debated now is to what extent and for whose benefit the bureaucracy makes policy. For some observers, the policy making ability of the bureaucracy is omnipresent and excessive. In their provocative assault on the excesses of government, Milton and Rose Friedman write that contemporary bureaucracy is pervasive and beyond control of policy makers and the public alike: "Higher-level bureaucrats are past masters at the art of using red tape to delay and defeat proposals they do not favor; of issuing rules and regulations as 'interpretations' of laws that in fact subtly, or sometimes crudely, alter their thrust; of dragging their feet in administering those parts of laws of which they disapprove, while pressing on with those that they favor."[40]

Other observers argue that bureaucrats are necessary to complement the workings of other public policy makers, particularly those in the legislative branch. Bureaucrats, write Ripley and Franklin, "make numerous decisions in the course of administering their programs that are important to members of Congress. . . . [But] bureaucrats cannot exercise the power they have over expenditures, location of facilities, or expansion or reduction of services, without to the political repercussions such exercise of power has in Congress."[41] Thus, in this view, the bureaucracy is a vital component of the policy making process.

Whether their powers are modest or substantial, harmful or beneficial, skillfully utilized or politically exploited, bureaucracies are indisputable policy making actors in contemporary American society. To be sure, some bureaucracies are more independent than others; moreover, policy making abilities and limitations vary among bureaucracies. These shades of difference notwithstanding, modern bureaucracies must be acknowledged as far more than implementing agents or neutral functionaries for others. They are players in the policy making process.

Voting Public

Thus far, the policy making actor descriptions have had nearly universal application at various levels of public authority in the American polity. Indeed, wherever governments exist, chief executives—whether they are known as presidents, as governors, or as mayors—are part of the public policy mix. Similar conclusions may be reached about legislatures, courts, and bureaucracies—all function as vibrant policy making units at the national, the state, and the local levels of power.

Yet, there is at least one policy making component that does not have the widespread role discussed above. When acting as a collective body, the electorates in twenty-four states may exercise a policy making role at the state and local levels through reliance on the initiative. Primarily a political phenomenon rooted disproportionately in Western states, the initiative permits the public to formulate policy by adopting measures that citizens place on the ballot. State requirements for qualifying initiatives vary from a few thousand signatures to 10 percent of the electorate, but these differences do not seem to have a negative impact on initiatives in their petition stages. Such efforts are routine in the states that permit policy making by the voters. As Jeffrey Stonecash notes, the use of initiatives "may not be a primary means of making decisions, but it does occur regularly and does involve important concerns."[42]

The list of initiative policy areas is almost endless. Within the past decade alone, the voters in various states have acted on legislative term limits, abortion rules, minimum prison sentences for serious offenders, utility regulations, numerous forms of gambling (from bingo to riverboat casinos), handgun controls, affirmative action, immigration, legalization of marijuana for medicinal purposes, and dozens of other controversial topics. Particularly in states where it is used often, the initiative works as an alternative policy making process that circumvents the power of elected officials.[43]

In recent years, citizens in states where legislatures were unable or unwilling to pass policies have placed growing numbers of controversial initiatives on the ballot. Some of these efforts touched on minor themes, such as the 1994 initiative in Washington State in which voters approved the right of individuals to purchase dentures directly from manufacturers rather than through their dentists. Others have been incredibly costly battles, such as the 1996 struggle in California over the liberalized right of stockholders to sue corporations, a battle in which opponents raised more than $30 million to defeat the measure. And that wasn't even the record; in the 1988 struggle for insurance reform in California, the insurance industry raised and spent $75 million on a losing cause.

Of significance is that a substantial number of initiatives under consideration by the voters go down to defeat or are declared unconstitutional by state or federal courts. Defeat often occurs because of the complexity that initiative designers attach to their proposals, leading voters to feel more confused than assuaged. In California, for example, of 232 proposed initiatives that appeared on the ballot between 1912 and 1994, a full two-thirds were defeated by the electorate, even though many were well-financed efforts.[44] In addition, even initiatives that have captured public approval have ultimately been declared unconstitutional by state or federal courts. Thus, although voters in twenty-three states enacted term limits for their members of Congress between 1990 and 1994, those efforts were swept aside by the U.S. States Supreme Court in 1995 as unconstitutional. Constitutionality of outcomes notwithstanding, the initiative remains an important vehicle for those who seek policy changes but feel thwarted in their efforts to use traditional channels.

Policy Making Actors—Society's Power Brokers

While the policy making process may seem cumbersome and opaque, the cast of policy makers responsible for decisions is fairly observable. That key decision makers are identified, however, does not suggest that they will do what they have been chosen to do—cooperate in the construction of public policies. In order to predict policy maker behavior with any sense of certainty, we would require extensive information on leaders' values, interest group pressures, citizens' attitudes, institutional checks, and countless other factors that affect power and its exercise. Nevertheless, a catalog of policy makers serves a useful purpose: it sensitizes us to the actors, and to the potential power of those actors, at the center of the public policy process.

Today's decision makers operate under conditions that are different from those of other eras. Historically, from the assemblies of Athens to the town hall meetings of New England, those who made policy had substantial direct contact with those who were affected by it. The makeup of modern society, however, is such that individuals are discouraged from attempting to make policy on every important issue; nor are they interested. With the exception of a few pressing matters decided in initiative states, we have learned to defer to a series of accountable leaders, an important break with the past. E.E. Schattschneider put the matter best, nearly forty years ago, when he wrote, "The problem is not how 180 million Aristotles can run a democracy, but how can we organize a political community of 180 million people so that it remains sensitive to their needs. . . .

The emphasis is on the role of leadership and organization in a democracy."[45] In other words, it is not practical for people to govern themselves in a complex society. Instead, democracy is determined through leadership choices. Likewise, public policies are thrashed out either by actors selected through the democratic process or by individuals responsible to those actors.

Our fivefold description of policy making actors frames the major participants in the policy process. Lest we attach too much significance to any particular category, we should remember that commitments seldom are constructed by a single policy making authority. In fact, for the most part, the system is characterized by carefully designed interdependence and joint decision making. Such cooperation is commonly required between policy making institutions at the national level (i.e., Congress passes a law; the courts uphold it), and is usually expected from comparable authorities at lower levels of government (i.e., the Environmental Protection Agency orders new strip-mining procedures; state bureaucracies enforce them). Should the necessary cooperation among policy making authorities fail to take place either between comparable levels of authority (horizontally) or authoritatively from top to bottom (vertically), the most important issues may remain without resolution. However, should such policies survive the rigorous endurance tests described above, their official prescriptions will be satisfied only through implementation. We turn to implementation, the next major step in the policy process, in chapter 5.

Questions for Further Thought

1. Who are the major policy making actors? How do they convert competing claims into public policy commitments?

2. Congress and the president have different accountability issues from the issues that confront courts and bureaucrats. What makes the two groups unique? What are the costs and benefits of these different arrangements?

3. Which of the five policy making actors has the most independence? Which has the least? What are the consequences of these different levels of autonomy?

Suggested Readings

Erikson, Robert S., Gerald C. Wright, and John P. McIver, *Statehouse Democracy* (New York: Cambridge University Press, 1993).

Fisher, Louis, *The Politics of Shared Power*, 3d ed. (Washington, DC: CQ Press, 1993).

Gilmour, Robert S., and Alexis A. Halley, eds., *Who Makes Public Policy?* (Chatham, NJ: Chatham House, 1994).

Glick, Henry R., *Courts, Politics, and Justice*, 2d ed. (New York: McGraw-Hill, 1988).

Stoesz, David, *Small Change: Domestic Policy under the Clinton Presidency* (White Plains, NY: Longman, 1996).

Thurow, Lester C., *The Zero-Sum Society* (New York: Basic Books, 1980).

Van Beek, Stephen D. *Post-Passage Politics: Bicameral Resolution in Congress* (Pittsburgh: University of Pittsburgh Press), 1995.

Vogler, David J., *The Politics of Congress*, 6th ed. (Madison, WI: Brown and Benchmark, 1993.

5 IMPLEMENTATION: CONVERTING POLICY COMMITMENTS INTO PRACTICE

Public policies are responses to new goals, new values, and new relationships that emerge out of crises and confrontations. Simply said, public policies are commitments to something. As instruments of decision makers, however, policies do not *institute* movement as much as they *direct* movement. In order for policies to work, appropriate government agencies must undertake the process of converting new laws and programs into practice. *Implementation represents the conscious conversion of policy plans into reality.* It is the "follow-through" component of the public policy making process.

At first glance, it may seem that implementation activities are an automatic continuation of directives orchestrated by government institutions and decision-making authorities. Nevertheless, there often exists a substantial gap between the passage of new laws or rules and their application. This gap can cause havoc with the policy making process.

A famous U.S. Supreme Court decision illustrates the difficulties that can accompany implementation. In its ruling on the *Cherokee Nation v. Georgia* case of 1831, Chief Justice John Marshall and his colleagues decided by a 6 to 2 vote that the state of Georgia had illegally seized some Indian lands.[1] As a result of this, as well as a subsequent case, the Court ordered President Andrew Jackson to protect the rights of the Cherokee tribe.[2] In defiance of the Court's action, President Jackson refused to accept its opinions. Chief Justice Marshall strongly implied, in turn, that "it was the President's duty to uphold the appellant's rights under federal law," to which admonition Jackson is reputed to have replied, "John Marshall has made his decision; now let him enforce it."[3]

The reluctance of an assigned government unit to carry out the legal directive of another unit shows the tentative state of implementation. There is no natural law ensuring that the policy adopted today will be carried out as intended tomorrow. Indeed, the relationship between decision making and implementation is tenuous at best.

Even though implementation is toward the back side of the decision-making process, policy execution inevitably depends upon the components of public policy that precede it. The policy making process is somewhat akin to the physical composition of a chainlink fence, with its weblike fingers that connect and overlap other sections of the structure. The anatomy of a chainlink fence suggests two distinctly different interpretations of its utility. In one sense, much material seems to be wasted, as one part of the chain curls around another, with the excess suggesting little more than decorative value. In another sense, the fence is organized in such a manner that the various parts of the chain are interdependent. Thus, a single link, while unimpressive alone, is simultaneously the extension of one section and the partial foundation of another. This complementary design provides continuity and, hence, the unexpected strength of the chainlink fence.

Policy implementation reveals the strengths and weaknesses of the decision-making process. Like a chainlink fence, implementation relies on connections for its purposes and direction. The primary connecting elements include triggering mechanisms, a public agenda, and the attempted resolution of emergent issues. These are linked to decision makers who take into consideration various policy alternatives. Policy decisions, in turn, are linked to various agencies and officials, who are assigned the task of executing the new policies. At this point, the implementation of policy faces a range of possible outcomes that include intentional obstruction, inefficiency, neglect, and synchronized cooperation. At some point in the future, all that has or has not been carried out will be scrutinized through a process known as evaluation, the subject of chapter 6.

While implementation signifies the completion of the policy cycle in one sense, it may well represent the beginning of new policies as well. Poorly designed and poorly executed policies may create new triggering mechanisms. However, well-written, successfully implemented policies may put a long-festering public issue to rest. Depending on a variety of circumstances pertinent to an issue, the links of the public policy fence can be direct and strong or fragmented and weak. And implementation is a major part of the material in that fence. This chapter begins with an explanation of the implementation framework and its relevance to the public policy process. As with other components of policy making, implementation rarely works in an absolute manner. In the pages that follow, we will discuss some of the major nuances associated with implementation. Among these are the extent to which a policy is carried out (implementation by degree); the kinds of governments that are responsible for managing a new policy (microimplementation versus macroimplementation); and the power of the principal government entity that must do the implementing (the bureaucracy). Inasmuch as implementation constitutes the last major component of a policy, it is important to understand those factors that encourage or prevent its occurrence. Finally, this chapter focuses on the inducements as well as the obstacles to policy implementation. Here a host of variables determine how well the crucial important step in the policy making process converts rhetoric into reality.

The Implementation Framework

Implementation represents the effort to put the policy making effort into place. Positioned on the less visible "backend" of the process, this component is often overlooked and undervalued, with less knowledgeable observers believing that decisions are automatically put into effect. Yet, the fact remains that official enactments by appropriate government agencies and institutions are little more than statements of intent without successful adoption. If you visualize a seesaw with policy formulation at one end, implementation is the balance on the other side. As Michael Hayes writes, implementation "consists primarily of the execution of policy."[4] Without an application consistent with its intent, policy has neither substance nor significance. Policy success depends on how well bureaucratic structures implement government decisions.

Until recently, even most learned observers tended to overlook the value of implementation. With their focus mostly on major policy institutions such as the presidency, Congress, and perhaps, the courts, observers tracked public policy from their points of emergence in the political system to the moment of adoption. Major scholarly works emphasized the values and compromises that shaped policy as those crucial to the workings of the governmental process.[5] Viewed retrospectively by one policy analyst, early treatments of the political process were so caught up with the descriptions of government offices that they failed to consider either the outcomes of institutional decisions or the ways in which commitments were converted into activities.[6] As a result, considerable confusion developed when policy applications varied from policy commitments. One of the concerns of contemporary political science, then, has been to trace policy from its origins to implementation and, with the help of evaluation (see chapter 6), to actually determine the extent of congruity from the beginning to the end of the policy cycle.

Efforts to understand and evaluate policy implementation have been hindered by the low visibility of the bureaucracy, the most commonly utilized agent of the implementation task. Most policy makers (i.e., the president and Congress) face a good deal of public scrutiny because of their consistent accountability to the public. Many are confronted with periodic public assessments of their efforts in the form of elections, press reports, or criticisms from other political camps. Yet, the decisions of policy makers are actually carried out by bureaucratic agencies with little direct accountability to the public. Randall Ripley and Grace Franklin conclude that "The bottom line with reference to delegation of authority is that a good deal of the detail of public policy is made by the bureaucracy," even though the core of the policy making process is located in the more visible parts of government such as Congress or the presidency.[7] The failure of bureaucratic agencies to implement a policy properly not only brings confusion to the intent of the policy but also helps to rekindle the political debate initially responsible for the policy action.

In addition to their relative invisibility, bureaucracies often have tremendous latitude in the means and methods they use to carry out their assigned tasks. Such discretion varies with the type or level of bureaucracy and the form of public policy that the bureaucrat is assigned to carry out.[8] Given the lack of standardized procedures and conditions for implementing public policies, it is easy to understand the confusion about bureaucratic behavior; there are few generalizations with respect to predictable action. The implementation process of one bureaucracy may be strict or narrow, while the implementation effort of another may be filled with flexibility. Why such inconsistency? The answer, writes James Lester and Joseph Stewart, is because those who formulate policies "are often unable or unwilling to include precise guidelines due to the complexity of an issue under consideration or because of lack of time."[9] Nevertheless, the combination of general public awareness and the vast amount of discretionary power makes bureaucracies sleeping giants in the public policy making process.

As we have ascertained in the first few chapters of this book, the policy making process is fraught with challenges and obstacles; implementation, the final step of policy decisions, suffers from similar difficulties. In actuality, the policy decision itself may be the last opportunity for legislation to be recognized in its entirety. Once adopted, a policy is dissected by multiple interpretations, assessments, and responses—some in concert, others in contradiction—by both the bureaucratic sector and other levels of government. As Charles Lindblom notes, "The mere size of the government's efforts at administering or implementing of policy poses staggering problems of resolving conflict and of arranging cooperation."[10] The largesse of government at the national level obviates Lindblom's comments. Difficulties with respect to implementation can be found at other levels of government as well, even with small units such as cities, where the carrying out of policy directives "requires a considerable investment of executive resources—assuming the mayor *has* such resources—to direct implementation of programs under the mayor's leadership."[11] Only the process of evaluation (see chapter 6), an activity that takes place subsequent to a policy's operation, gives any sense of where and how the policy has been implemented vis-à-vis the intentions of those who designed it.

While some disagreement exists over the elements that compose implementation, certain assumption seems to have widespread acceptance. For implementation to occur:

1. There must be an *entity with sufficient resources* assigned to carry out the implementation task.
2. The implementing agency must be able to *translate goals* into an operational framework.
3. The entity assigned the implementing task must *deliver on its assignment and be accountable* for its actions.[12]

Identification of the components necessary for implementation in no way is a barometer of success; such awareness only points to the myriad of hurdles that must be overcome en route to fulfilling a policy objective. For a variety of reasons outlined later in this chapter, the same agencies that successfully implement one policy may fail in their efforts to implement another policy of similar design or structure. Such inconsistency stems from the complex processes that determine implementation objectives and strategies for individual policies.

Bureaucracies as Agencies for Implementation

Bureaucracies are the necessary, if sometimes cumbersome, outgrowths of modern government organization. As institutions and their responsibilities have become more complex, bureaucracies have been established to carry out government-directed objectives. Kenneth Meier writes, "When faced with acute crises, chronic problems, or even apathy, the positive state [government] responds; and the response usually includes a bureaucracy."[13] Thus, when the national government adopted a policy to secure the environment from decay, the Environmental Protection Agency was established to administer this new goal. Similarly, when Congress decided that armed services veterans needed an agency to look out for their issues, the Department of Veterans Affairs, a new cabinet post, was created to carry out this objective. To a large extent, bureaucratic agencies are the responses—and are supposed to respond—to the directions of public policies.

Although designed chiefly as *policy implementing agencies*, bureaucracies often assume *policy making* roles. In the words of one authority, the difference between policy making and policy administration often is "clearer in theory than in practice. In highly complex societies, bureaucratic organizations often are asked to elaborate alternative approaches to a problem in addition to translating a policy into concrete programs and implementing those programs."[14] Such enhancements add to the responsibility of the bureaucracy, often giving it much more power than its designers ever intended.

Sometimes bureaucracies are pared back because policy makers perceive that these administrative entities have become inefficient or no longer necessary. Thus, when the newly elected Republican-dominated Congress sought to eliminate the Department of Commerce in 1995, its motivation was largely guided by the feeling that the Cabinet was more harmful than beneficial to the promotion of U.S. commerce. On other occasions, policy makers have attempted to eliminate bureaucracies that have either assumed or been given too much power. Republican

Speaker of the House of Representatives Newt Gingrich expressed such sentiment about the Food and Drug Administration in 1995 when he referred to the agency as "the leading job killer in America," thereby touching off yet another round of debate on the merits of the agency as a health guarantor versus an obstacle to business.[15]

Creation of the Medicare system exemplifies how a bureaucracy can simultaneously thrive, yet become threatened in a sea of controversy. Medicare was developed by Congress in 1965 as a "pay-as-you-go" medical health program for the elderly who were eligible for Social Security. For the first twenty years of its existence, Medicare took in as much in taxes as it spent in benefits or more.[16] The program fulfilled the needs of a major population segment. But then large numbers of people began living longer, leading to greater than expected demands on the Medicare fund. Based on these trends, a 1993 government report predicted that the Medicare fund would be broke by 1998 unless Congress acted to control soaring health costs.[17] With the costs of Medicare at $175 billion in 1993 and growing at twice the rate of inflation, congressional leaders took aim at the program, which was serving almost forty million people in 1995. In an effort to return the program to a "pay-as-you-go" basis, Congress basically halved the rate of future government funding for Medicare, suggesting a bleak future for recipients. President Clinton, protesting that congressional leaders were going back on their commitment to protect the elderly, vetoed the bill. But, to look beyond the specifics, the clash over Medicare illustrated the concerns of those who worried about out-of-control costs pitted against the fears of others that America was breaking its word to senior citizens.

Implementation by Degree

The mere decision to create a policy or a law in no way dictates any certainty of application. Sometimes the wheels of government move at a slow pace; moreover, with our congested system of actors and tasks, sometimes the wheels stop altogether. But for *any* movement to occur, compliance and cooperation are required at all levels in the policy framework, from government agencies to individual citizens. Given the public's general acceptance of government, it is a rare occasion when those wheels grind to a halt. It is another matter, however, to assert with confidence that all government policies are implemented with their intentions intact. More times than not, implementation is not a "yes or no" matter. Rather, it is an activity that occurs in degrees.

One way of understanding the potential for implementation is to examine the extent to which different *types* of policies are carried out. Theodore Lowi divides public policies into three separate categories: distributive, regulatory, and redistributive.[18] *Distributive* policies have had a long-established role in American politics. These policies are designed to ensure that government decisions benefit specific clientele. Once identified chiefly as patronage appointments and contracts, distributive policies now respond to the demands of society's major sectors—especially labor; business; agriculture; and, most recently, armed services veterans. The need for government to accommodate these groups became so great that Cabinet positions were structured within the executive branch to ensure a smooth policy flow from planning to implementation.

Regulatory and redistributive policies are both products of the New Deal era. According to Lowi, it was during the Great Depression that Congress delegated its lawmaking authority "increasingly in statute after statute to an agency in the Executive Branch or to the president, who had the power to subdelegate to an agency."[19] These policies were designed in such ways that Congress would pass laws and would delegate to others the ability to "fill in the details." Lowi labels such delegation "administrative legislation"; it gives bureaucratic agencies broad discretion to implement laws as they see fit.

There are, however, certain differences between regulatory and redistributive policies. It is the overt intent of *regulatory* policies to award special benefits and opportunities to select clientele. General rules are applied by administrative units on a case-by-case basis. Agencies such as the Federal Communications Commission and the Interstate Commerce Commission are known for exercising regulatory powers. For example, when the licenses of radio and television stations must be renewed, the FCC determines their merits by examining the arguments relevant to a single station or owner, with no need to do so on a comparative basis. Some critics argue that the implementation of these powers can be arbitrary, if not discriminatory.[20]

Unlike regulatory policies that maintain special ongoing relationships, *redistributive* policies have wide application in the political process. Inasmuch as they account for the largest portions of the national domestic budget, redistributive policy impacts are particularly vital to sizable sectors of society who get more from government than they put in. Taxation and welfare programs are examples of redistributive policies. Their controversy is demonstrated by the political costs to President George Bush of the Budget Reform Act of 1990 (a tax increase of $500 million was enacted after a pledge to do otherwise) and the dip in President Bill Clinton's popularity after his ill-fated attempt to alter welfare policy in 1994.[21]

Lowi's analysis represents substantially more than a division of public policies—it provides a guide to which policies are likely to be implemented with precision and which are not. This throws a spotlight on the objectives of policy makers and, at least, raises the possibility that some policies are implemented as intended, while the fates of others are more ambiguous. Such suspicions of inconsistency and misdirection become more pronounced when Lowi's framework is used to assess the extent to which bureaucracies manage policy implementation. Here we may observe a wide range of relationships between policy intent and policy administration.

In his study of the federal bureaucracy, Kenneth Meier discovered that discretionary powers of relevant agencies that deal with the three public policy areas varied greatly. While distributive policies are implemented with some bureaucratic discretion, Meier noted that appropriate Congressional subcommittees and those organized groups receiving distributive benefits exercise continuous oversight. Given these checks, distributive agencies tend to implement policies in accordance with the needs of their clientele.[22]

With respect to regulatory policies, most agencies are responsive to the community over which they preside. Although regulatory agencies theoretically follow congressional guidelines, the independence given to them allows them to be discretionary in their work. A case in point is the changing role of the Environmental Protection Agency, which was originally set up by President Richard Nixon in 1970 as an independent pollution control agency with particular concerns for air and water contamination.[23] Yet, over time the agency's administrators expanded its functions considerably. For example, in 1993, the EPA declared that "passive" or secondary tobacco smoke was a human carcinogen. Although the EPA had no mandate to determine workplace or restaurant conditions, its ruling on the secondary smoke issue provoked nationwide changes in companies to create nonsmoking environments in order to avoid lawsuits by victims of cancer and other illnesses brought on by passive smoke.[24]

In the area of redistributive policy, little discretion is left to bureau-crats. Because of the partisan importance of such redistributive areas as income distribution, welfare, health, and housing, Congress is very precise with regard to managing these policy commitments. In Meier's words, "Congress perceives redistributive issues as so important that they should be resolved in the legislative branch rather than by the bureaus in consort with their clientele."[25] Although the massive na-tures of such policies act as barriers to new policy directions, the implementation is fairly routine and reflective of the intent of policy makers.

As the foregoing suggests, implementation is anything but an all-or-nothing process. Some laws encourage precise implementation, while others do not; some policy changes leave room for bureaucratic ma-neuvering, while others transpire under the scrutiny of their makers. It is often the case that implementation does not occur wholesale, but by degree.

To some extent, implementation success can be predicted by the policy area in question. Nevertheless, in light of the important role implementation plays in the political process and the different circum-stances under which it may or may not occur, the public policy analyst must examine a policy change from its inception as an issue to the point where it is applied as law or new rule.

Vertical Versus Horizontal Implementation:
Adventures in Federalism

Implementation efforts may move between levels of government and/or within levels of government. Indeed, the requirements of feder-alism, the multifaceted web of intergovernmental relations, make it likely that most public policies will be implemented by a series of institutions or levels of government.[26] At the same time, the im-plementation process will be encouraged or discouraged, in part, by the route of policy application.

If Congress passes a national law that requires administration solely by an agency in the executive branch, the horizontal path may limit the number of actors as well as increase synchronization. Creation of the Resolution Trust Corporation in 1988 serves as a case in point. Virtu-ally all activities associated with the stabilization of the banking indus-try—from funding to oversight—took place at the national level. With no vertical linkages for the Resolution Trust Corporation, its activities remained closely tied to (and monitored by) Congress.

On the other hand, when one or more segments of the national government must interact with institutions at other levels on the federal ladder, the implementation challenges increase. No issue better exemplifies vertical difficulties than the question of civil rights. The U.S. Supreme Court declared racial discrimination unconstitutional with a unanimous 9 to 0 decision in 1954, and ordered state and local governments to change conditions as necessary.[27] Nevertheless, vestiges of state and local resistance to the Court's decision continue to this day. A study forty years after the historic decision showed that two-thirds of all minority children still attended minority schools; relatedly, a national survey revealed that sizable majorities of both whites and blacks favored efforts to strengthen neighborhood schools over integration.[28]

As a public policy increases in complexity and in layers of interaction, its implementation activities may transcend both the vertical and the horizontal dimensions of bureaucracy and the political process. With each new dimension of government involvement, the policy faces a new power base, a different set of interpretations, and the potential of resource scarcity. Because of the hazards associated with implementation of overlapping institutions and levels of government, the coordination issues can become as compelling the policy itself.

Conditions that Promote Implementation

Because different political actors and institutions are connected with each policy, the implementation framework varies with each public policy enactment that awaits execution. Moreover, the opportunities—both structural and political—to halt, delay, or modify policy commitments are numerous. For now, however, we focus on the conditions that can facilitate the implementation effort. Some of the more valuable of these inducements include adequate funding, boilerplate provisions, limitations on the number of agencies involved, and political controls on the bureaucracy.

Funding

Few provisions are as vital to the ultimate achievement of a public policy goal as funding. Adequate financial resources allow for making long-term plans, making staff arrangements, making policies operational, and completing policy objectives. Most of all, funding is the hallmark of commitment.

Consider the Food Stamp program, proposed by President Lyndon Johnson as part of his "War on Poverty" effort during the mid-1960s. Johnson argued that putting an end to hunger represented the first step toward ending poverty in America, and in 1964 Congress responded to Johnson's plea by passing the Food Stamp Act. The program allowed recipients to purchase food coupons at a fraction of their worth; the coupons could then be redeemed for food at nearby supermarkets or food outlets. The Food Stamp program began with an initial budget of $400 million for two million recipients. By 1994, twenty-seven million people—more than one out of ten Americans—received benefits totaling $26.4 billion. Part of the program's expansion has been due to the increased numbers of eligible people who receive food stamps. Between 1989 and 1992 alone, the number of participants among those eligible grew from 56 percent to 69 percent. With increasing recipients and federal dollars for the Food Stamp program, criticisms have become more vocal as well. By 1996, both President Clinton and the Republican Congress agreed to trim about one million recipients from the Food Stamp program, but fundamental differences in political values made substantive changes all but impossible.[29]

When a policy commitment represents a restructuring of values rather than the direct transfusion of public monies from one set of needs to another, funds still may be required to guarantee implementation of the new policy. Such was the case when the United States decided to join more than 120 other nations as a signatory to the General Agreement on Tariffs and Trade (GATT) in 1994. Although the financial costs were relatively minor losses to the U.S. treasury, American participation in GATT represented benefits to some industries (movie making, agriculture, aircraft manufacturing, and computer software design) and problems for others (particularly garments and textiles).[30]

As the examples cited above indicate, funding is a key to making policy decisions work. Without funding, planning, coordination, and application all will be in vain. Yet, funding can be tricky, particularly if one level of government creates a policy that other levels must fund. The concept, known as *unfunded mandates*, was applied vigorously during the Reagan administration. Couched as "deregulation," "privatization," and "decentralization," this approach to policy making emphasized the notion of federal rules and state and/or local government application. Most distressing to the lower levels of authority were the excessive costs mandated upon them by the federal statutes.[31] The essence of legislative mandating was that it gave the illusion of smaller federal government while shifting responsibilities to other levels of government. Over time, this method of policy making drew increased anger from state and local authorities. Finally, the issue was addressed in 1995, when Congress and President Clinton enacted legislation that eliminated the unfunded mandates except under extraordinary circumstances. From this point on, federal programs would carry with them federal resources.

Boilerplate Provisions

Public policies sometimes are written in such a manner that their implementation is contingent upon the agreement of state and local government agencies or recipients in the private sector to a series of previously established conditions. Known as *boilerplate provisions*, these conditions represent commitments to general social goals created through programs adopted at earlier points in time. The implementation of one policy, then, may be dependent upon the continued enforcement of other laws or regulations.

Boilerplate provisions are particularly vital to those governments that rely upon federal financial assistance for support of their own programs. The numbers of dollars at stake are substantial. For the 1994–95 fiscal year, states and local governments received $217 billion in federal grants-in-aid, up from $97 billion in 1984–85. In many cases, these dollars amount to as much as 25 percent of a state's entire budget.

But the dollars are delivered on "terms." These conditions range from promises that the recipient agency will hire X percent racial minority or female contractors to the guarantee that it will hire all eligible workers for a specific program irrespective of their ages. Should the recipient agency fail to live by the boilerplate provisions associated with the grant-in-aid, in all likelihood it would lose its federal assistance, even if those funds were used properly for the program in question. Many of the nation's most visible public policies are linked with boilerplate provisions at the implementation stage.

The particular boilerplate conditions built into a specific public policy may be completely unrelated to the new program designed for implementation. Moreover, according to one study, these strings have increased with allocations of federal dollars.[32] The combination of strings and growing federal financial commitments has led many observers to take a hard look at the grant-in-aid concept.

Current reassessments notwithstanding, boilerplate provisions remain as subtle, yet powerful components of policy implementation. Their importance lies not only with the specific legislation to which they are connected, but with general commitments made at previous points in the public policy making process. Simply put, their conditions help to assure that new policies are carried out simultaneously with the fulfillment of long-standing goals.

Limited Numbers of Agencies

American government is a maze of overlapping and interconnecting policy making structures. Horizontally, at the national level, executive, legislative, judicial, regulatory, and (to some extent) bureaucratic entities both compete for and share authority. Similar divisions of authority not only occur at the state and local levels, but also must interact with the power that flows from the national sector. Given these myriad points of pressure and influence, it is easy to see the challenge of implementation. Recognizing this framework, Robert Lineberry offers the following observation: "The larger the number of actors and agencies involved, the lower the probability of successful implementation."[33] But there is another side to Lineberry's axiom: Restated in a positive context, this logic holds that successful implementation depends upon simplicity, and simplicity demands that authority and administrative responsibilities be shared among the fewest possible agencies.

Development of the interstate highway system in the United States demonstrates the success that can be attained from a program that has limited numbers of participants. Initially designed in 1944, the network is scheduled for completion by the century's end. When fully operational, the interstate highway grid will contain 44,000 miles of four-lane (at least), high-speed roads. Estimated cost for the project is $129 billion, but the potential payoff seems substantial: with 1 percent of the roadways in the nation, the efficient interstate system will carry more than 20 percent of the traffic. Significant for this discussion is that the system has been built with tight vertical management. Under the auspices of the Department of Transportation (DOT), the federal government pays 90 percent of the cost and supplies standards. State highway department counterparts pick up the rest of the tab and build the roads.

Political Controls on the Bureaucracy

Bureaucracies are important components of the political process because they translate orders, laws, and decisions into concrete application. In carrying out their assigned tasks, however, bureaucracies rely largely upon their own biases and interpretations. This self-appointed control mechanism is known as *bureaucratic discretion*. It is important because the implementing approach determined by bureaucrats can be just as vital as the content of the policy itself. As Charles Jones notes, "The policy process relies heavily on the communication of words and their meaning. Interpretation—'What did they mean by that?'—is crucial to understanding what goes on at every stage of decision making."[34] Somewhere, somehow policy makers and policy implementers must be on the same page.

Without political controls on the bureaucracy, implementation of the intended policy may drift away from policy objectives. Marc Landy and his colleagues discovered this problem in their exhaustive examination of the Environmental Protection Agency. In its effort to meet confusing mandates and directives, the authors explain, the agency "has ignored gray areas, fuzzy boundaries, and ambiguities; sorting situations instead into a small number of distinct, mutually exclusive boxes."[35] As a result, the public and the policy makers have been confused by some of the EPA's actions, thereby harming the agency's credibility.[36]

But controls on the bureaucracy need not only occur from within the internal bureaucratic apparatus. If policy makers expect accurate implementation of their goals, their participation in the policy making process must continue beyond the point at which decisions are made. Robert Lineberry cites several strategies that policy makers may use to assure that their commitments are carried out as intended. These include:

1. *Change the law* to tighten loopholes that bureaucracies use for discretionary authority.

2. *Overrule the bureaucracy* through the powers that exist in the presidency or cabinet level officials.
3. *Transfer responsibility for administration elsewhere* so that new bureaucrats will be more respectful of actual policy commitments.
4. *Replace a recalcitrant agency head* when the current official in charge repeatedly thwarts clear legislative, executive, or judicial intent.
5. *Cut* if there is no way to assert control over the agency's management practices.
6. *Abolish the agency altogether* if there is no other way to assert control over the agency's management practices.
7. *Make the legislation more detailed* to force the bureaucracy into conformity with specific instructions and narrow laws.[37]

With proper oversight, it is much more difficult for bureaucracies to exercise discretionary authority in a manner different from the policy's design. Members of the executive branch can supervise implementation through tight controls of cabinet agencies and occasional executive orders where appropriate; legislators can oversee implementation through watchdog committees and the power of the purse; even judges can affect implementation by issuing new court orders, although, admittedly, their power to control bureaucracies is less than that of other government branches. Why don't these policy makers exercise such power with greater regularity? Perhaps because such bold action would result in higher visibility (and greater controversy) than they might like.[38] Nevertheless, political control of the bureaucracy remains the most effect means by which to guarantee precise implementation.

Conditions that Obstruct Implementation

Clear, specific, and well-directed policy decisions are essential prerequisites for implementation. Even so, the prospects of either implementation failure or partial implementation haunt the public policy making process. Some of the most critical obstacles include bargaining, lack of funds, changes in priorities, multiple goals, and poor oversight.

Bargaining

Bargaining has a different character in public policy implementation than it has during the period of policy creation. As part of the decision-making process, which includes compromise, bargaining is a commonly accepted ingredient of politics. With respect to implementation, however, the time to discuss the merits of various policy proposals theoretically is over. Since only a small portion of the many political actors who make the policy are also involved in its application, further debate would cloud the original issue and obstruct completion of the original public policy objective.

Once a public policy decision has been made, the need for exact application is paramount if it is to reflect credibly upon the policy and policy makers alike. Nevertheless, bureaucrats are often allowed to bargain, or to negotiate, as a means of smoothing out any unforeseen problems connected with implementation. The more an implementing agency is allowed to bargain, the more likely it is that the policy in question may be administered in an arbitrary way. While bargaining may make life easier for the bureaucracy, it decreases the value of policy and law.

In his discussion of "interest-group liberalism" as the modus operandi of implementation, Theodore Lowi refers to bargaining as one of the reasons for the decay of modern American government. As government's role has expanded, administrative agencies have been given discretion to implement policies. In Lowi's words, "delegation has been elevated to the highest of virtues, and standards have been relegated to the wastebasket of history because that is the logic of interest-group liberalism. Bargaining ... must be preferred over authority at every level and phase of government."[39] With bargaining as an administrative tool, public policy implementation takes place on a case-by-case basis. Because the bureaucracy often implements decisions with an eye to expedience, a single public policy casts a different shadow with each application. Bureaucrats, then, act less as administrators and more as politicians charged with the responsibility of policy making. Each implementation effort becomes unique with each set of circumstances, leaving the "policy" a meaningless description.

Because of pockets of criticism in the Clean Air Act Amendments of 1990, considerable after-the-fact bargaining has taken place between the EPA and affected groups. Much of the discussion has occurred as part of the movement toward less regulation. Thus, in 1995, for example, EPA Administrator Carol Browner announced special regulations for companies with 100 or fewer employees that violated environmental regulations. Browner stipulated that small companies would be given six months to correct their environmental abuses, even though the legislation contained no such specific provision.[40] What Browner described as an attempt to ease regulatory burdens was nothing other than a rewriting of law through postlegislative bargaining activity.

Bargaining may be viewed as a subtle obstacle to implementation; however, bureaucrats do not always employ it successfully. This is because bargaining activity between an agency and an interested party may be related not only to the design of a specific policy but to the clout of the implementing agency and the issue under review. For example, Gary Bryner finds that bargaining is likely to be intense in those policy areas in which a relatively narrow sector of society is called upon to pay for the benefits enjoyed by many (e.g., environment, health, or safety regulation); conversely, bargaining will not be intense when the benefits of a policy are narrowly focused and the costs are spread among a broad base (e.g., price supports, tariffs, or licensing).[41] Depending upon the policy area and the affected parties, bargaining can be a major roadblock to the implementation of a policy per its intentions or design.

Lack of Funding

As discussed earlier in the chapter, funding is a critical ingredient in the implementation of public policy commitments. Therefore, the absence of adequate financial resources can undermine the objectives set forth by decision makers. If necessary, monies do not accompany (or follow soon after) a public policy commitment, the policy objective is likely to suffer in some proportion to the absence of funds. It may seem contradictory for a decision-making authority to decide upon a commitment without suitable resources for implementation. Nevertheless, such ironies are part of the political process.

In some instances, policy making agents intend to fund their programs but fail because of political breakdown, or because of a fierce struggle over resources after the program's passage. The underfinanced EPA Superfund constitutes a case in point. As enacted in 1980, the Comprehensive Environmental Response Compensation and Liability Act set aside $1.6 billion over a five-year period to deal with toxic waste, oil spills, and other hazardous sites in need of restoration. Nevertheless, twelve years and $13 billion later, only 60 of 1,275 sites had been repaired, and EPA officials estimated eventual site repair costs of $700 billion![42] Clearly, this policy area was underfunded with respect to the objectives it was designed to meet.

In other instances, a policy may fail to garner funds because of a conflict between the actors in two or more institutions which share responsibility for creation of a public policy. One such battle occurred between President Clinton and Congress in 1993. En route to his victory, Clinton proposed a massive community service program for 150,000 high school graduates who, as a condition of their two-year commitment, would receive a modest stipend and enough money for four years worth of college tuition. By the time Congress worked over the idea, only enough dollars were in the program to permit a fraction of the number to participate in a program that would provide two years worth of education.[43]

Simply stated, inadequate funding is a virtual guarantee of programmatic disaster at the point of implementation. If a program lacks the necessary resources, or if competing arenas of power disagree on the necessary commitment, substantial amounts of policy making energy may be wasted.

Changes in Priorities

Abrupt policy changes are not commonplace in American politics. Political traditions and long-term, well-defined relationships among policy makers, bureaucrats, and powerful interest groups generally work against rapid change in the policy arena. This is not to suggest that the public agenda is static or unyielding. However, policy makers are more likely to alter existing commitments in subtle, piecemeal fashion than through wholesale change.

Despite this tendency toward incrementalism, or slow change, dramatic new demands or events occasionally lead policy makers to respond with new commitments. At these points in the decision making process, one long-standing public policy may be replaced by another, or an existing commitment may be dropped without replacement. New directions in public values can, in fact, bring implementation of existing programs to an abrupt halt.

The election of a conservative Republican Congress in 1994 stands as a dramatic event which precipitated attempts to alter the courses of numerous policy traditions in American politics. Prior to the election, then-Minority Leader Newt Gingrich and 300 Republican candidates for the House of Representatives stood on the House steps and pledged loyalty to their "Contract with America." When the dust settled from the election, Republicans emerged as the majority party in both houses of Congress for the first time in forty years, and work on the Contract began in earnest. Some of the elements in the Contract, namely unfunded mandates and new employment rules for Congress, secured quick victory in the Congress and concurrence of President Clinton. Other, more controversial items, such as a proposed balanced budget amendment, just missed securing the necessary votes for passage. A third category, ranging from abortion restrictions to tax cuts, encountered both the wrath and the veto of President Clinton. In the end, the most controversial elements of the Contract with America failed to clear the presidential veto hurdle, setting up the conditions for confrontation in 1996.

Despite the logjam of key Contract elements, the document established new terms for doing business in American politics. Talk no longer centered on incremental expansion of Social Security or the 600-plus grant-in-aid programs annually enacted and reenacted by Congress. Instead, debate shifted to how much would be cut, what responsibilities would remain with the government, and who would be at fault if the new policies failed. Indeed, President Clinton, himself, moved to consolidate 271 federal housing, transportation, training, and health programs into 27 broad state-administered grants, showing the extent to which even he was affected by the 1994 election results.[44] As a result, one assessment concluded, the U.S. government changed course and began "redesigning what it built precisely thirty years ago" under Lyndon Johnson's "Great Society."[45]

Rarely do changes in priorities occur with the impact of the Republican wave of 1995. But when they do take place, such alterations have the capability of directing policy makers in a different direction.

Multiple Goals

Public policies often are pieced together as coalition products, the result of intense negotiating and compromise among several political actors. As policies are subjected to many pressures, they may appear to be hybrid compilations born out of conflict. Because of the complex negotiations along the path to adoption, a new policy, therefore, may stress several goals simultaneously as the price for keeping an ad hoc coalition intact.

The need to satisfy multiple goals may be the political price for organizing seemingly incompatible ideas into a workable public policy decision. Point of fact, recent changes notwithstanding, the Food Stamp program's longevity is explained in large part because it met more than one goal: while the program availed food stuffs to a large number of poor people at a nominal cost, it provided price supports and sources of stability for the agricultural community; furthermore, the assurances that sizable quantities of food would be taken off the market guaranteed minimum surplus slack, thereby assuring a relatively tight market and strong prices for growers. Given the benefits to so many segments of society, the program met with little resistance. But once the issue of welfare reform became a centerpiece of the new Republican majority, even the multifaceted Food Stamp program was not beyond reproach; and given the Republican demand of "less government," it became impossible to sustain the various objectives of the policy.

Although adopting multiple goals may be a political necessity in order to assure a policy's passage, incomplete coordination of competing objectives into compatible goals can bring on implementation failure. In some instances, for example, the conflicting objectives of two government branches can have negative effects on policy application. In other cases, the objectives of national policy makers and local recipient agencies may be so divergent that policy implementation falls short of either group's goals.

The development, operation, and reconsideration of the nuclear power industry illustrate how multiple goals can paralyze a sector of the economy and leave society at risk. Nuclear energy plants initially were developed with the encouragement of the U.S. government during the 1950s and 1960s. By the 1970s, more than 100 nuclear plants were in operation or under construction, with an equal number in the planning stage. Proponents viewed these facilities as fulfilling goals relating to energy conservation, clean energy, and the promise of "cheap" power. Over time, it became clear that nuclear energy plants presented negative impacts, too, particularly with respect to possible accidents and contamination. The 1979 accident at Three Mile Island, Pennsylvania, followed by the 1986 Russian meltdown in Chernobyl, contributed greatly to fears of nuclear disaster. Suddenly, it became clear that some of the objectives related to nuclear energy, foremost among them a healthy environment, were at risk. By the 1990s, the nuclear industry was in shambles, partly because of broken faith and partly because of the uncertainty within government regulatory agencies.[46] As opponents moved to terminate the generation of power from these units, their concerns were compounded by the tremendous costs associated with decommissioning nuclear plants—costs that actually exceeded construction and all other benefits of the plants.[47]

Contemporary public policies are replete with the problems like those connected with nuclear energy policy. As the number of objectives increases, the likelihood grows that not all objectives will be satisfied. Such discontent leads to a breakdown in implementation and, potentially, to reconsideration of the policy in question.

Poor Congressional Oversight

As has been noted elsewhere in this volume, public policy emerges from many government sectors. Quite often, the policy making process integrates several levels of public authority and more than one branch of government before the commitment has been carried out. Of the various policy making institutions, the legislative level—particularly the U.S. Congress—is unique because of its involvement in the policy process at several critical junctures, including implementation. Congressional oversight represents the process of scrutinizing the implementation of policy decisions. Nevertheless, Congress has a spotty record in exercising this authority. Once a policy has been enacted, Congress often takes only a cursory glance at its outcome; instead, it places such responsibilities in the hands of the bureaucracy. Lack of congressional supervision often hinders implementation.

As the grand "committee of committees," Congress divides itself into three dozen committees and more than 200 subcommittees. It is this specialization that allows members of the legislative branch to develop expertise in relatively narrow policy areas. At the same time, specialization of members of Congress has a negative by-product, fragmentation. Narrow subcommittee responsibilities give members of Congress the opportunity to become familiar with small niches rather than with the general policy area that ultimately gets treated by the full committee and Congress as a whole. With responsibilities so divided, control over what happens to policy is almost impossible. In the view of one study, "the highly dispersed nature of oversight responsibility, the lack of strong oversight committees, and the natural conflict among committees all undermine severely the ability of Congress to conduct serious, rational control of administration."[48] Thus, the fruits of Congress's labor are often harvested with little congressional control.

Why has Congress failed to exercise its oversight function? As the demands on numerous policy fronts have increased, Congress has tended to deal with the "big picture" while relinquishing broad discretionary authority to bureaucratic agencies. More often than not, congressional laws seemingly have sent the following message to the bureaucracy: "Okay, we've given you the concept; now it's up to you to make it work." Implementation is what "makes it work," yet bureaucratic interpretations of policy intentions may be radically different from those of congressional policy makers.

In recent years, Congress has attempted to reassert its oversight authority by including the *legislative veto* as part of its lawmaking arsenal. With the legislative veto, Congress gives the bureaucracy broad responsibility for carrying out legislation, but reserves the ultimate authority to approve or disapprove the actual implementation effort. Much of this approach was undermined in 1983, when the U.S. Supreme Court ruled that it was unconstitutional.[49]

Congressional oversight increased a notch in 1995 under the leadership of new House Speaker Newt Gingrich. Bearing in mind a 1994 campaign promise to balance the budget within seven years, Republican majorities in both houses ushered through a rescission bill. This bill eliminated $16.4 billion in federal spending that had been already committed for the 1994–95 fiscal year. The spending-cut areas included education, housing, job training, environmental protection, and President Clinton's already decimated National Service volunteer program, along with several controversial provisions described by President Clinton and Democratic critics as "pork," or unnecessary pet projects. Ultimately, the president first used his veto power against this bill,[50] and Congress failed to muster the necessary two-thirds vote in each House to overturn the president's veto.

The struggle between Democrat Bill Clinton and the Republican Congress continued throughout the 104th Congress. Although the Congress prided itself on flexing its oversight muscles, some critics argued that such actions were more a matter of reducing government and scrutinizing policy administration.[51]

Implementation: Link or Lapse in the Public Policy Process?

Enactment of a public policy makes implementation possible. Nevertheless, although the latter cannot take place without the former, the simple sequence is by no means certain. In a sense, each policy commitment can be compared to a seedling planted in a garden. The seedling has the potential of undergoing great physical change, the outcome from which may result in a shade-bearing tree or a full-grown plant. Once placed in the ground, however, the seedling requires water, nutrition, and cultivation if it is to grow as intended. Leaving the seedling to chance without any intervention would make the future of the young plant uncertain.

So it is with implementation. The policy decision is an important, vital ingredient for programmatic response. Public policies are shaped by studies, demands, problems, and other elements which are subsequently translated into commitments by government institutions and actors. But policy enactment alone does not guarantee that implementation will be consistent with its objectives. Policies must be properly structured, funded, and directed so that the implementing bureaucracy has a clear framework for application. In other words, for policies to succeed, clear lines of transmission and jurisdiction must be drawn. Thus, policy makers have to be precise, while bureaucratic discretionary authority must be constrained. In addition, implementation requires willing cooperation by relevant actors and institutions along critical intersections of the federal network.

Regardless of the inducements for implementation, public policies often will be applied more by degree than in entirety. Incomplete implementation clouds the public policy process for both decision makers and the public. Such confusion frequently undermines the credibility of those individuals responsible for the public policy.

Implementation depends upon the linkage between policy makers and bureaucrats for its success. To this end, Kenneth Meier writes that public policy "is no longer so simple that the legislative decrees are self-implementing. The complexities of modern public policy demand functions that can only be performed by large scale formal organizations,"[52] namely bureaucracies. However, despite the indispensability of bureaucracies as facilitators of implementation, they unquestionably complicate the public policy making process. As hierarchical organizations, bureaucracies are structured to make policies work. But a problem develops when the policy maker expects the bureaucracy to make policy as well. Conflict then moves from the open environment to a closed environment, and resolution becomes vulnerable to the vagaries of interpretation.

Questions for Further Thought

1. What is the primary role of implementation in the policy making process?
2. Bureaucracies are crucial agencies for implementation, yet they are often criticized for what they do. What is behind this seeming inconsistency?
3. It has been written that, more times than not, implementation takes place along the lines of a continuum. What does this mean? How can the chances for implementation of a public policy be maximized?

Suggested Reading

Aberbach, Joel D., *Keeping Watchful Eye: The Politics of Congressional Oversight* (Washington, DC: Brookings Institution, 1990).

Craig, Barbara Hinkson, *The Legislative Veto: Congressional Control of Regulation* (Boulder, CO: Westview, 1983).

Gerston, Larry N., Cynthia Fraleigh, and Robert Schwab, *The Deregulated Society* (Pacific Grove, CA: Brooks/Cole, 1988).

Goggin, Malcolm L., Ann O'M. Bowman, Lames P. Lester, and Laurence J. O'Toole, Jr., *Implementation Theory and Practice* (Glenview, IL: Harper/Collins, 1990).

Harris, Richard A., and Sidney M. Milkis, *The Politics of Regulatory Change: A Tale of Two Agencies* (New York: Oxford University Press, 1989).

Nakamura, Robert T., and Frank Smallwood, *The Politics of Policy Implementation* (New York: St. Martin's Press, 1980).

Reagan, Michael D., *Regulation: The Politics of Policy* (Boston: Little, Brown, 1987).

Stoker, Robert P., *Reluctant Partners: Implementing Federal Policy* (Pittsburgh: University of Pittsburgh Press, 1991).

Walker, David B., *Toward a Functioning Federalism* (Cambridge, MA: Winthrop, 1981).

Wildavsky, Aaron, *The New Politics of the Budgetary Process* (Glenview, IL: Scott, Foresman, 1988).

6 EVALUATION: ASSESSMENTS AND DIRECTIONS

If there is an underside, or a stealthlike component, of the public policy process, it lies with the process of policy evaluation. So much political capital is directed toward agenda building, formulation, and (to a lesser extent) implementation of a public policy that we often overlook the most obvious review questions of all: Did the new policy attain its stated objectives? What levels of satisfaction or dissatisfaction developed as a result of the new policy? Has implementation of one policy created in its wake additional issues for the public agenda? Policy evaluation is the activity devoted to answering these questions.

Simply defined, *policy evaluation assesses the effectiveness of a public policy in terms of its perceived intentions and results.* Policy makers spend a good deal of their time and political capitol framing what they *want* to occur. But the essence of evaluation, Lawrence Mohr writes, exists in comparing "what did happen after implementing the program with what would have happened had the program not been implemented."[1] As such, policy evaluation is a reactive experience that takes place in the aftermath of an earlier activity. It is the best opportunity for those parties interested in the public policy process to glean firsthand knowledge about whether a commitment has been carried out in line with its design. Other than internal assessments or unexpected events, it is also the last major opportunity to bring the policy back into the decision-making arena if it has been mismanaged, or if it has had undesirable impacts or unintentional consequences. Policy evaluation is a powerful tool of the policy making process because of its potential to reframe an issue once thought to be resolved by policy makers.

Like other components of the policy making process, the meaning of evaluation has evolved over time. During the 1950s and 1960s,

when the practice of evaluation was first developed as a formal component of policy making, analysts went out of their way to "measure"
results without regard to values.[2] At that time, practitioners viewed
evaluation as a narrow quantitative mechanism for scientifically measuring the outcome of public policy implementation. Such objectives
are somewhat limited, by today's standards.

In recent years, the evaluation focus has changed. A number of
contemporary authorities in the evaluation field now argue that it is
nearly impossible to separate policy assessments from the values that
go into the policies as well as from the political environment that
surrounds the implementation of policies. Thus, Dennis Palumbo and
Steven Maynard-Moody conclude, "All evaluations are political in the
sense that they are commissioned by individuals with a political stake
in their outcome, they are fed into a political decision-making process,
and they take a stand on program success or failure."[3] In today's world
of complex decisions and multifaceted application, policy evaluations
have decidedly quantitative *and* qualitative elements; accordingly, they
are more comprehensive assessments of those policy applications.

Contemporary policy evaluation now looms as a vital element in the
arsenal of activities associated with judging what governments decide
to do and the value of what they have done. Particularly in democracies, policy evaluation provides a check on the merits of the policy
making commitment and subsequent implementation. Without this
mechanism, we may have little sense of whether budgets have been
spent correctly, rules have been applied as written, or individuals have
carried out their assignments as directed. Evaluation not only allows
analysts to compare the "before" and "after" elements of the policy
making process, but also offers the opportunity to assess the outcomes
of what has or has not been put into place. In other words, without
policy evaluation, both the credibility of the policy and the accountability of those individuals and institutions responsible for its development remain uncertain.

Such concerns have more than mere intellectual or abstract value. In
fact, they speak to the compelling question of legitimate authority.
Why should anyone approve the organization of a program or the
spending of public monies unless he or she believes that the proposal
will be carried out as presented? We know from the information discussed elsewhere in this volume that the time period between design
and implementation can be prohibitively long. We also know that both

the number of individuals and the number of institutions associated with a given policy can be many, and at times unwieldy, and that large numbers of participants in the formulation component increase not only the complexity but the likelihood of implementation problems. All these conditions present potential challenges to the execution of a public policy commitment.

Policy evaluation provides feedback to what has occurred and the extent to which the commitment has been fulfilled as intended. As such, it assists in a review of whether authoritative actions have been carried out appropriately within their legally defined framework, as well as in evaluating other issues surrounding that framework. With its emergence in the "back end" of the public policy framework, evaluation has become an important element of the policy making process.

This chapter zeroes in on the various ingredients of public policy evaluation. Specifically, we examine the evaluation environment, the major approaches to policy evaluation, the types of analyses that emerge in their wake, and the options that may be considered when sufficient information permits additional action steps.

One final note: Like all the other elements of the public policy process, evaluation, too, is an inherently *political* activity. "Objective" tasks notwithstanding, evaluators begin and end their work with their own values, criteria, and objectives, sometimes determining the impact of a policy with less than detached standards. Such actions do not necessarily doom the value of the evaluation experience as long as we are able to acknowledge and deal with these biases as part of the chemistry known as *evaluation.*

The Evaluation Environment

In its most basic context, evaluation represents the attempt to gather information about a public policy that has been put into place. The circumstances of and conditions related to that information-gathering experience, however, are critical to the credibility of the conclusions that are reached and, ultimately, inserted into the public policy making framework. If the evaluation takes into consideration intent, implementation, and the intervening factors that may separate the two elements, then the conclusions are likely to provide helpful insights. However, if an evaluation is little more than a knee-jerk response to a policy unpopular with the evaluator, then the analysis represents little more than a crass political statement.

Some experts argue that it is virtually impossible to separate clinical assessments from the larger, social, value-laden framework. Thus, policy deliberation, Frank Fischer writes, "works on two fundamental levels, one concretely concerned with a program, its participants, and the specific problem situation to which the program is applied, and the other concerned with the more abstract level of the societal system within which the programmatic action takes place."[4] To the extent that the process stays on the first track, evaluators are likely to be more rule-oriented in their assessments. To the extent that the process follows the second track, evaluators will be more normative in their reviews.

There are several key criteria associated with the policy evaluation objective. They include: assignment of an agency or political institution with the responsibility of performing the evaluation effort; determination of the rationale for assessing the worth of the policy that has been formulated and implemented; ownership of sufficient resources to fully execute the evaluation effort; and an authority designated to receive the information resulting from the evaluation enterprise. In the public sector, most evaluation activities are assigned by one government body to another, although some public entities specifically include independent evaluation by outside authorities as part of their ongoing activities.

Why Evaluate?

Once a public policy is implemented, decision makers and casual observers alike may wonder if it is working as intended by those who enacted it in the first place. Such curiosity is likely to be much more than an academic exercise. A new policy may cost considerable dollars or may present the potential of rearranging key values; accordingly, the more there is at risk, the more important it is to go through evaluation.

Policy or program evaluations may also serve to distinguish perceptions of success or failure from reality. By benchmarking a condition and measuring subsequent change, an evaluator or evaluation team may reach conclusions significantly different from knee-jerk assessments.

Often, reactions to a new policy may be far more serious than the initial conditions that made way for the policy. In other words, implementation of a program may go beyond its objectives as defined by policy makers. Under such circumstances, analysis and measurement of the outcomes are vital not only to the policy's future but to other elements of the public policy making environment. Such work may also help policy makers realize that they need to go "back to the drawing board."

Evaluation of public policy for critically ill newborns illustrates the problem that a policy in one area can produce for others. During the Reagan administration, pro-life groups joined with disability rights organizations in an effort to pressure the government to develop strict policies regarding the treatment of severely retarded or deformed babies. Proponents were particularly worried about infants suffering from spina bifida and Downs' syndrome. Until that time, physicians had been left to work out solutions with parents on an ad hoc basis. By the mid-1980s, the Reagan administration was threatening sanctions against hospitals that "interfered" with the right to life of deformed babies. In fact, effective in 1984, the administration published a series of government guidelines to protect handicapped babies. Yet, the decisions to save the lives of deformed babies in the name of humanitarianism caused other problems for parents and physicians who, suddenly, were without their own rights. Robert Blank and Janna Merrick thus wrote of a large number of actors that the Reagan administration ignored en route to its pro-baby policy. They include physicians, medical technicians, attorneys, researchers, sperm and ova donors, and parents. The fact is, they note, that policies such as that promulgated by the Reagan administration caused even more difficulties for those involved in the issue.[5] Such conclusions were reached through careful evaluation of the stated objectives and outcomes of the administration's newborn programs.

Who Evaluates?

On a personal basis, almost everyone evaluates how he or she is affected by a policy. When taxes go up, for example, we not only deal with the change but judge the merit of that change. When the president commits troops to a remote part of the world, we not only watch to see whether the mission succeeds, but we also deliberate whether the move is desirable. But in the world of policy making, evaluation is often a formal component of the policy making environment, and is generally conducted by experts who are intimately familiar with processes and objectives pertaining to the issue undergoing assessment. Under these circumstances, evaluation is undertaken with deliberation and precision.

The selection of the evaluation agent or body is critical to not only the caliber of work performed but the credibility of the agent's conclusions. Those organizations that participate in the evaluation process because of their roles within the governmental process are known as *internal evaluators*. As official government organizations, they are likely to know about the policy and its nuances firsthand; these bodies are also so close to the political process that they may not be able or willing to demonstrate political independence from the policy making authority.[6] Thus, the Congressional Budget Office (CBO) is closest to (and probably most aware of) the efforts of Congress to meet budget targets; yet, the agency may be unnecessarily forgiving because of its proximity to Congress and its dependence upon the legislative branch for its very existence.[7]

More removed from the immediate policy making arena are *external evaluators*, independent organizations that are not officially attached to the policy in question but that, nevertheless, possess—or claim to possess—some expertise for reaching credible assessments.[8] External evaluators often do not have the political baggage of proximity to the policy making body or the implementing agency. On the other hand, they may be too removed from, and therefore insensitive to the nuances of the policies that they have been asked to assess.

Sometimes, groups that are either partially or totally removed from the public policy process will offer their evaluations of existing policies. For example, the National Industrial Conference Board offers monthly assessments of the health of the nation's economy. Completely removed from all public and private institutions, this group of university economists evaluates the direction of the U.S. economy by measuring several factors. When its findings are released, key policy makers tend to heed the Board's words simply because it *is not* affiliated with a bank, a brokerage house, an interest group, or any other element that might have a direct stake in the governmental process.

In other instances, interest groups may present themselves as independent, external evaluators, even though their existence is based on little more than a check on undesirable public policy initiatives. The Council for Tobacco Research, for example, has defined itself as an independent group tasked with evaluating the tobacco policies promulgated by the Food and Drug Administration. Yet, most industry observers describe the council as little more than a "front" for the tobacco industry.[9]

The difficulty here is the appearance of outsiders as independent, disinterested parties, when they may be quite the opposite. In such circumstances, they may well turn "evaluation" into a political exercise that centers on the value of the idea or policy proposal more than on the way it has been carried out, rendering their efforts little more than sophisticated interest group activity.

Whatever their distance from government, external evaluators are not without their own biases. And whether the evaluators are internal or external, the conclusions they reach may be the first step toward the organization of a future public policy endeavor.

Approaches to Evaluation—Process versus Outcomes

Public policies may be evaluated in terms of their process as well as their outcomes. *Process* refers to the means by which a policy is carried out. With this evaluation approach, the evaluator focuses upon whether the policy has been executed as intended by those who have framed it. *Outcome* evaluations center on the actual change that has taken place from the time of the policy's formation through the period of its implementation. Outcome evaluations deal with qualitative assessments. Whether the difference is perceived or real, the extent of change is important for determining the benefits that may have accrued as a result of the policy's implementation. Ideally, process and outcomes evaluations should be conducted as sequential activities, although the absence of resources or the presence of a political agenda may lead the evaluator to utilize only one tool.

Process

Process evaluation (sometimes known as *monitoring*) represents a systematic attempt by the participant to estimate the level at which a policy reaches those it is supposed to affect. This method, Peter Rossi and Howard Freeman note, "consists of measuring the degree of congruence between the plan for providing services and treatments (program elements) and the ways they are actually provided."[10] Process evaluation is not concerned with the quality, success, or value of the public policy as much as with the extent to which the implementation reflects earlier-stated objectives. As such, it is very specific in approach and precise in methodology.

Deregulation of the financial services industry serves as an example of a law that was carried out per the intentions of public policy makers, although their intentions may not have been well thought out. In order to relieve financial institutions of burdensome regulatory oversight, Congress enacted the Depository Institutions Deregulation and Monetary Control Act of 1980 and the Garn–St. Germain Depository Institutions Act. The deregulatory efforts spawned disaster for the industry and for investors, leading to hundreds of bank and savings and loan failures, as well as a $500 billion bailout price tag for the federal government.[11]

Quality Assurance

Once exclusively a tool of business management, quality assurance has emerged as an evaluation tool of the public policy making community. Like other evaluation tools, this process focuses on whether the needs of the customer have been satisfied by the policy that has been put in place. However, with quality assurance, the evaluator examines results on an ongoing basis, allowing for assessments to take place closer to the time of implementation as well as at periodic intervals after the event. Often, quality assurance is assigned to a team of evaluators who pursue their responsibilities by observations, interviews, and other means of data collection. The more consistent the application, the more successful the public policy. In other words, if the policy actually does what it is supposed to do—that is to say, functions per its intentions—then it works.

Biotechnology, a relatively new area of science that relies upon technology to alter the biological environment, has been subject to considerable quality control by government agencies. For years, scientists have attempted to improve the human condition through "genetic engineering," a process that permits sophisticated technologies to rearrange DNA and other biological components in such a way as to eliminate disease, neurological disorders, and other genetic deficiencies. The potential for the betterment of human kind as a result of this research is almost limitless; conversely, the possibility of using such research in a harmful way is also real. In order to make sure that genetic engineering abuses do not take place, the National Institutes of Health (NIH), an agency of the federal government, routinely establishes and monitors guidelines for biotechnological research and development.[12] While such efforts do not guarantee compliance, they set the tone (and some controls) for standards and compliance in the industry.

Measuring Change

Perhaps the most demonstrable indication of implementation is observed by comparing the results of a policy with the original conditions that inspired it. Quantitative measurement of change permits such analysis, providing readily understandable data for appraisal. Unlike qualitative assessments, the analysis of change based on percentages, on the addition or loss of variables, or on "before" and "after" comparisons invites straightforward comprehension by a broad-based audience. As an element of process evaluation, measurement focuses not only on the merit of change but on the extent to which it has occurred.

The Clean Air Act of 1970 illustrates the extent to which a policy may satisfy some goals while failing to meet others; either way, the nature of the law invites measurement as a means for assessing success or failure. The law was put into place over the course of more than two decades. A few components were carried out in concert with intentions, although implementation of some elements extended beyond the original deadlines. In other instances, implementation of the Clean Air Act made little headway, according to independent assessments of the efforts by the Environmental Protection Agency.[13] Such measurement served as the basis for subsequent legislation enacted by the Congress in 1995.

Outcomes

Whereas process evaluations deal with the extent to which policies are carried out as intended, outcomes evaluations emphasize the quality of the implementation. At stake here is whether what actually happens is good or bad, right or wrong, worth the investment or not worth the price. Outcomes evaluations are particularly important, because the findings may well point the way toward continuing that which has already been done or toward reconsideration of a policy newly in place. With outcomes assessments, the policy analyst has the opportunity to recast an issue on the public agenda, thereby starting the public policy making process anew. The two best-known forms of outcomes evaluation are cost-benefit analysis and experimental research.

Cost-Benefit Analysis

Cost-benefit analysis is an accountant's dream! This method of evaluation provides a means by which the policy analyst ascertains the effectiveness of a new program in terms of resources expended and dividends gained. The cost-benefit approach deals with the narrow issue of worth; at the same time, it may be applied broadly to areas outside the immediate area of a policy's application. Assuming that a new policy initiative is put into place exactly as intended, and that the results match expectations of its sponsors, the question remains, is the policy worth the cost and expense? In other words, are we getting our money's worth, compared to alternative approaches or methods? This is the essence of cost-benefit analysis. A new program may satisfy its stated objectives in the immediate sense, but be burdensome or unpredictably expensive nonetheless. This is where cost-benefit analysis is a valuable tool; it considers all elements relevant to the implementation of a new policy, allowing the analyst to weigh the merits of the policy in the widest possible context.

Examination of the Endangered Species Act represents a case in point. The law, originally passed in 1973, provides a safety net for animals and plants that are near extinction by preventing human intrusion into their endangered habitats. More than a gratuitous gesture to animals, the act emphasizes the links of the life chain; more than 900 animals and plants have been listed as "endangered" by the U.S. Fish and Wildlife Service. As fulfillment of the law's mandate, landowners in affected areas are required to provide comprehensive development plans for agency approval. Critics have condemned these requirements for their costs in money and time. A former Interior Department official complained, "the Fish and Wildlife Service has no incentive at all to figure out ways to cheaply provide habitat, when they instead can in effect condemn huge acreage with the stroke of a pen, at no cost."[14] Several members of Congress have since begun to reconsider the Endangered Species Act not because of the law's failure, but because of the costs associated with unintended consequences.

Another recent policy change subjected to the rigors of cost-benefit analysis was the adoption of a new federal minimum wage law. Studies conducted by the Clinton administration and several leading economists all concluded that the new law, which increased hourly wages by 90 cents over a two-year period, would have little impact on businesses and workers. Most persuasive was a study of an 80-cent-per-hour increase in the state of New Jersey, one of ten such states with minimum wage levels above the federal level. The study, along with two dozen other similar efforts, found "insignificant evidence of job loss." Such information, occurring under conditions similar to the would-be federal change, proved powerful ammunition for federal minimum wage law proponents.[15]

Experimental Research

In some instances, the assumptions and applications of a policy may be tested through the efforts of experimental or exploratory research.[16] Under such circumstances, scientists and other experts focus on the claims that led to sponsorship of a policy. Such efforts include examination of targeted groups (elements singled out for scrutiny or policy impact), random sampling, pretest/posttest comparisons, and intervention.[17] Experimental research often validates previous assumptions, putting to rest claims to the contrary. Sometimes, however, new findings may lead policy makers to reassess the merits of an ongoing program, thereby placing a once-resolved issue or set of questions back onto the public agenda.

Efforts to understand the linkages between smoking and lung cancer illustrate the power of experimental research as well as the consequences of its findings with respect to current policies and future implications. Lung cancer is a serious disease; with more than 170,000 new cases diagnosed every year, it is the leading cause of cancer deaths in the United States. For more than forty years, government and university researchers have suspected tobacco as a cause of cancer, although their findings have been viewed by industry defenders as incomplete and indirect.[18] In 1996, using complex statistical studies on human subjects, scientists in Texas and California discovered the particular cigarette smoke ingredient that is responsible for causing lung cancer as well as the mechanics that precipitate ensuing genetic damage. The results of the research, leading scientists claimed, called into question government policies regarding tobacco industry practices. In addition, the new data threatened to alter outcomes from the growing number of court cases that have generally left tobacco companies off the hook as parties responsible for premature deaths of smokers.[19]

Metaevaluation

Along with defining evaluation in terms of process and outcomes, the evaluation concept itself may be subject to "evaluation." This approach, referred to as *metaevaluation,* represents the effort of an evaluator to assess the assumptions and procedures relating to the data that has been collected for analysis. If the value of gathered information is suspect or tainted, then the worth of the analysis is also brought into question. To put it another way, metaevaluation provides the opportunity for an evaluator to validate approaches, methodologies, and various hypotheses that form the foundations of the conclusions reached by experts charged with assessing a program or policy.[20] It may also serve as a check for policy makers who might otherwise act on false assumptions.

Evaluation of the evaluations associated with immigration policy indicates the extent to which different analytical approaches regarding the same issue can yield decidedly different assessments and future policy recommendations. Experts on all sides of the issue conclude that California has more illegal immigrants than any other state—perhaps as many as three million. This consensus notwithstanding, considerable disagreement exists over whether illegal immigrants contribute more or less to the economy than the cost of the benefits they receive from government agencies and services. In one recent study of California, the evaluator concluded that illegal immigrants cost California $5 billion more than they pay in taxes, and that they have displaced more than 900,000 Californians from their jobs.[21] A separate study concluded that the typical illegal immigrant actually contributes nearly $8,000 more in taxes than he or she receives in benefits over a lifetime. Assuming three million immigrants living to age seventy, these data would suggest additional tax income of $3.4 billion per year.[22]

How can studies of the same group yield such different results? In each case, the evaluators reached their conclusions by relying upon their own sets of assumptions. In the first instance, the data did not reflect the purchase power of illegal immigrants and the benefits from their participation in the economy; in the second instance, the study did not clearly separate legal immigrants from illegal immigrants. Adding to the confusion is the fact that, historically, neither the U.S. Census Bureau nor any other official government agency asks people their legal status—a question forbidden by federal law. Because of the confusion that arises from these various sources, evaluators have been stumped over which data are most relevant on the immigration issue, leaving those on all sides of the issue to pick and choose data as they please.[23]

Metaevaluation cannot resolve different conclusions such as those described above. However, this evaluative process can illustrate the problems associated with inconsistent approaches and potentially flawed assumptions. With this assistance, analysts and policy makers have the opportunity to continue examination of controversial issues instead of moving forward with commitments based on flawed data. Such pause may go far in providing reason for a cautious reassessment among those associated with implementation of a program or policy.

**Evaluation and Public Policy Making—
Using the End as a Beginning**

Although it comes at the end of the policy making cycle, evaluation can be viewed as the foundation for new policies; conversely, evaluation may serve as confirmation of policies that work. Whatever its impact, evaluation provides assessments about the policies that have been debated, formulated, and implemented. Referring to the systems approach to politics described by David Easton forty years ago, evaluation provides "feedback" for those who make public policy.[24] At a time when cynicism abounds in American politics, such linkage is a valuable way of connecting those who make change with the impact of that change.

But evaluation increasingly addresses another group as well. In the age of delegation, bureaucrats and administrators have increasing responsibilities for determining policy choices as making those policies work, moving, as Frank Fischer notes, ever closer to the "center of the decision making process."[25] As such, more than ever, evaluators have a pivotal role in the public policy framework. To this end, Ronald Sylvia and his colleagues have developed a ten-point checklist for policy evaluators. Summarized, the list components are as follows:

1. Is the program experimental or ongoing?
2. Who is the audience for the evaluation?
3. Are the evaluation methods appropriate for the audience?
4. What kind of evaluation is desired?

5. What is the purpose of the evaluation?
6. What kinds of data are necessary for the evaluation?
7. How will the information from the evaluation be used?
8. Are there sufficient resources to carry out the evaluation?
9. Will the evaluation measure the right elements?
10. Who will care about the evaluation results and why?[26]

Most of the time, evaluators do not make public policies. Nevertheless, their assessments are often close to the policies and those who do make them. With this in mind, evaluation has taken its place as a vital element of the public policy process. Although evaluation may seem to be the "back door" of the policy making cycle, it also serves as the window for future policy making decisions.

Questions for Further Thought

1. Some observers describe evaluation as the "underside" or the "back end" of the public policy making process. What is meant by this claim? Why does it have or not have merit?

2. Process and outcomes are two primary approaches to evaluation. Using your knowledge, cite examples of recent public policies that have been evaluated by each of these methods.

3. Although far removed from the policy making process, evaluators nonetheless have the potential to impact the formulation of future policies. At the same time, evaluators are not elected and, therefore, are accountable to virtually no one. What do you make of this irony?

Suggested Reading

Bonser, Charles F., Eugene B. McGregor, Jr., and Clinton V. Oster, Jr., *Policy Choices and Public Action* (Englewood Cliffs, NJ: Prentice-Hall, 1995).

Fischer, Frank, *Evaluating Public Policy* (Chicago: Nelson-Hall, 1995).

Haas, Peter J., and J. Fred Springer, *Policy Research and Public Decisions: Concepts and Cases for Public Administration* (New York: Garland, 1997).

Meier, Kenneth J., *Politics and the Bureaucracy: Policymaking in the Fourth Branch of Government*, 3d ed. (Pacific Grove, CA: Brooks/Cole, 1993).

Mohr, Lawrence B., *Impact Analysis for Program Evaluation* (Pacific Grove, CA: Brooks/Cole, 1988).

Osborne, David, and Ted Gaebler, *Reinventing Government* (New York: Penguin, 1993).

Posavac, Emil J., and Raymond G. Caray, *Program Evaluation*, 3d ed. (Englewood Cliffs, NJ: Prentice-Hall, 1989).

Rossi, Peter H., and Howard E. Freeman, *Evaluation: A Systematic Approach*, 5th ed. (Newbury Park, CA: Sage, 1993).

Sylvia, Ronald D., Kathleen M. Sylvia, and Elizabeth M. Gunn, *Program Planning and Evaluation for the Public Manager* (Prospect Heights, IL: Waveland, 2nd ed, 1997).

7 POLICY MAKING IN AN EVOLUTIONARY CONTEXT

The invention of the movie camera by Thomas Edison in 1889 represented a great leap forward for the concept of storytelling. Prior to that moment, photographers were limited to "stills," pictures that showed their subjects in frozen positions. Such displays left the viewer without the ability to see the events before, after, and even during the time which the photographs were taken. Stated another way, still photography presented material in the context of a static environment.

Movies changed all that. With the ability to shoot and show frames in rapid sequence, photographers could depict action as well as unfolding events. This technological breakthrough gave photographers the means to chronicle circumstances and conditions in an entirely new and more informative (not to mention more entertaining) way. It's not that moviemaking invented storytelling; it's that moviemaking, as compared to still photography, represented a much more comprehensive and a much more creative approach to telling stories.

What does this have to do with the study of public policy making? Politics is a mainstay of life. Wherever there is a struggle for resources that do not exist in quantities sufficient for those who desire or require them, there will be politics. Likewise, whenever there is a dispute over values underlying the distribution of rewards and deprivations, there will be politics as well. It is the process of these struggles and their outcomes that directs us to the study of public policy. Just as motion picture photography has found a multi-dimensional way to present the kinds of stories that were once unveiled by still photographs, so it is that the study of public policy has emerged as an improved way of describing the interaction between political issues, actors, institutions, and society.

Expanding the Context

As chronicled here and elsewhere, public policy making is more than "government." Traditional descriptions of the utilization of power emphasized the interaction of formal authority relationships, telling us little about the development of issues, the ways in which they were managed, or the outcomes. Such chronicles tended to leave out much of the policy mix. To this extent, contemporary emphasis on political change permits discussion and analysis in a considerably larger framework than has been used in the past.

Utilization of a wider lens to study politics allows the analyst to appreciate the dynamics of the whole as well as its parts. More than ever, we realize that civil war in Somalia can impact policy making decisions in Washington; that breakthroughs in gene splicing can reframe an issue such as abortion, and that illegal immigration from Mexico can influence the public policy setting in states such as California and Texas, as well as at the national level.

Equally important, we recognize that actors in the policy making process are not only elected officials or designated public authorities. Sometimes they are seemingly nonpolitical people who suddenly find themselves in political situations. Consider the case of Marc Klaas, father of Polly Klaas, a twelve-year-old girl who was raped and killed by a repeated felon. Marc Klaas had no experience in the political arena; yet, after his daughter's death, he set up the Polly Klaas Foundation for Missing Children, became a national spokesperson for missing children's issues, and led the movement for passage of "three-strikes-and-you're-out" legislation that ensured long-term incarceration for repeat offenders.

Within the public policy making framework, we are able to see how once seemingly extraneous factors connect with political decision making as well as with the consequences of action or inaction related to those issues. Within the same context, we can appreciate the value of nonissues, potential political problems that are resolved before they reach the attention of the policy making environment. Such activities as "shuttle diplomacy," quiet efforts "behind the scenes" in hot spots around the world, occasionally appear as foreign policy examples. On the domestic front, the government guidelines on DNA research established by the National Institutes of Health as long ago as 1976 represented an early effort to prevent the mismanagement of genetic engineering.[1]

In addition to nonissues, there remains an array of potential issues that, for lack of immediate tragedy or triggering mechanism, would otherwise descend into the policy making arena with tremendous urgency. The tenuous condition of the nation's underground water system constitutes such an example.[2] More to the point, an understanding of the policy making process gives meaning to how and why such questions move from seemingly benign existence outside the policy making arena to active areas of concern.

Focusing on Process

By viewing the policy making arena as a dynamic, moving environment, we underscore its process orientation. The focus on process is important because it illustrates the ongoing nature of policy making. Actors, events, and conditions interact in often unpredictable ways, leading to equally unpredictable policy decisions and applications. The process goes on long after basic decisions are made. New actors and new pressures deal with implementation, while still others offer feedback on what has or has not been put into place. Throughout the entire cycle of events, countless political forces attempt to shape and reshape the issues working their way through the public policy making machinery. Thus, the welfare reform package hammered out by Congress and President Clinton in 1996 emerged in a much different form from its original design; furthermore, early indications of its implementation by the Clinton administration suggest an even more radical departure from the law signed by the president.

Of importance is the fact that while policy making is in itself an intensely political experience, the issues leading up to policy making decisions and application may or may not be developed initially in a political context. Consider the issue of "term limits," a concept that would allow the polity to set constraints on the length of service in elective office. This highly political question was debated extensively before and during the writing of the Constitution, and has been on the public agenda ever since.[3] At issue was (and is) the linkage between elections and representation. Between the late 1980s and the early 1990s, reformers in twenty-three states secured passage of congressional term limits as a way of forcing the turnover of elected officials. Nevertheless, the U.S. Supreme Court, in a 5 to 4 decision, declared in 1995 that such restrictions were "contrary to the fundamental principle of our representative democracy, embodied in the Constitution, that the people should choose whom they please to govern them."[4] Thus, the process surrounding the term limits debate has been political from the first debate to the present time.

At the other end of the spectrum are those issues that originate well outside the political arena but that, because of unanticipated events, are swept into the cauldron of the policy making process. The case of *E. coli* bacteria stands out as such an example. This little-known toxic, a by-product of cow excrement and fertilizers, interested only scientists until its presence in apple juice that caused the death of one person and the serious illness of fifty-four others. At issue was the fact that the apple juice had been processed without pasteurization, a traditional industry practice. With the bacteria crisis, in 1996, the Food and Drug Administration considered new pasteurization regulations designed to prevent the recurrence of the *E. coli* bacteria problem.

The examples above share a trait: namely, that policy making stems from a process that recognizes issues, organizes those issues into political and nonpolitical tracks, and sends the political issues into the decision-making arena for disposition, implementation, and evaluation. Those matters that stay out of the political context, say professional athletes' salaries or the evolution of language, remain outside the policy making arena because of the consensus that they do not require the intervention of public authority. The resolution of those matters that are political, or that become political, however, will take place via the policy making process.

Underscoring the Principles of Politics and Policy Making

In politics, change is constant. The overall public policy making framework is similar to a kaleidoscope's ever-changing picture arrangements in that it is in a state of perpetual transition. Some policies may remain in place for long periods of time, yet others will be forged, altered, or eliminated. It is uncertainty that brings such drama into the public policy making experience.

Ever-changing circumstances notwithstanding, public policy making is wedded to certain basic principles of politics. These staples include the existence of conflict, the public nature of an issue, the presence of decision makers with the ability and resources to resolve the issue, a commitment resulting from the debate to deal with the dispute, and some assessment of what is or is not done, and the extent to which the commitment fulfilled objectives. All these elements are far from antiseptic; rather, they are laced with political values.

Conflict as a Precursor

Disputes arise from disagreements over values and policies, and these arguments are the proving grounds of the policy making environment. The unfolding of such controversies may occur over time periods ranging from gradual development to sudden emergence, but their addition to the public agenda rearranges the entire constellation of issues on the public agenda. Some social scientists worry about excessive conflict in American society as a sign of dissolving consensus.[5] Others, however, conclude that not only are the divisions over values well managed, but also they bring out the best in society and public policy makers alike.[6] Why? Without some well-defined way to express conflict, disaffected elements of society might become increasingly contentious or alienated from the political process.

The Struggle over Defining Public Issues and Values

Where does one draw the line between public and private issues? This question is a key element in the politics of policy making and a critical activity for the policy maker. With respect to the work of Congress, for example, Edward Schneier and Bertram Gross note that several factors are important in establishing the boundaries between public and private issues and policies. Among these is the pivotal question, for whom? The more interested parties that are likely to benefit from a proposed policy, Schneier and Gross conclude, the more likely it is that the proposal will be transformed into policy.[7] Conversely, the more groups that are interested in a proposed policy, the more likely it is that pressures will appear on all sides of the policy issue, as policy makers attempt to find common ground for resolution. Nevertheless, the fundamental issue for the public and policy maker alike is to determine what issues are part of the public agenda.

Policy Makers as Managers of the Public Good

Throughout the policy making process, those who are part of the decision-making apparatus must act on behalf of the public. Policy makers may differ on the merits and/or benefits of a proposed policy, but their disputes must be about their interpretations of the public good, not the private benefit; this is the essence of leadership.[8] Equally important as substance is the process through which matters are decided. While it is important for conflicts to be resolved, it is almost as important that policy makers be seen attempting to resolve them. Such effort presents symbolic benefits as well as the possibility of resolution; if observers perceive an open, legitimate process at work, this alone will go far toward generating a sense of public inclusiveness in the political process. To this extent, the policy making process is a profound psychological component of the political system.

Execution of Decisions

Much of the value of a political system depends upon how authoritative power is exercised by those in power. Following through in a manner consistent with the "rules of the game" shows the polity that policy makers respect the system as much as they expect others to respect the system. Thomas Dye writes that if people believe that public policy makers carry out decisions according to the laws that have been prescribed, then they will "feel obliged to obey laws, follow rules, and abide by decisions that they believe to be legitimate." But if people question the legitimacy of decisions, then they will not feel compelled to accept them.[9] Elections offer voters the opportunity to assess, among other things, whether incumbents have performed as promised. If so, those already in office may be given further opportunities to govern; if not, they may be denied reelection for failing to follow through.

Evaluation of the Activity

Inasmuch as policy making focuses on the commitment of values and resources, the process must include some means of checking up on the decisions made and the way they have been executed. This evaluation component remains essential to the overall process for two reasons: first, because evaluation provides an opportunity to review the linkage from the origins of a policy to its implementation and, second, because such information provides potentially powerful feedback for the rest of the policy making network. Feedback represents closure of the policy making loop, allowing communication from those affected by a policy to those who put it into place. The very process orientation of public policy making must include mechanisms for such information transfer on a continuous basis.

Future Questions

The American political system is anything but a static arrangement of institutions, actors, and responsibilities. Quite to the contrary, it is open and susceptible to unexpected events and responses. The floodgates of the policy making arena rarely hold back the surges of concern, whether they stem from elements of the public, private individuals, the media, bureaucrats, or those actually in position to make decisions. In today's political environment, it is abundantly clear that the key to policy making is not whether information and concerns spill into the policy making arena, but the ways in which that information is successfully channeled, filtered, and managed with desirable outcomes.

As society becomes more complex, the rush of issues will only increasingly test limited resources and competing values. The policy making process is one way of understanding the means through which conflicting demands are heard, reconciled, and resolved in orderly, if not always satisfactory, fashion.

Questions for Further Thought

1. With the description of the process now complete, what do you believe is the greatest strength of the public policy making framework? What do you view as the greatest weakness?

2. Public policy making has been described as an evolutionary process. What factors contribute to this condition?

3. Conflict is at the heart of the public policy making experience. Give examples of a conflict-laden issue that has been successfully resolved as one that has remained on the public agenda without resolution. What factors were responsible for resolution of the first example, and what factors have impeded the unresolved issue?

Suggested Readings

Dye, Thomas R., *Power and Society*, 7th ed. (Belmont, CA: Wadsworth, 1995).

Hird, John A., ed., *Controversies in American Public Policy* (New York: St. Martin's Press, 1995).

Meenaghan, Thomas M., and Keith M. Kilty, *Policy Analysis and Research Technology* (Chicago: Lyceum, 1994).

Mills, Claudia, ed., *Values and Public Policy* (Fort Worth, TX: Harcourt, Brace, Jovanovich, 1992).

Wells, Donald T., and Chris R. Hamilton, *The Policy Puzzle* (Upper Saddle River, NJ: Prentice-Hall, 1996).

Woshinsky, Oliver H., *Culture and Politics* (Englewood Cliffs, NJ: Prentice-Hall, 1995).

NOTES

Notes to Chapter 1

1. For an example of early twentieth-century emphasis on institutions, see Woodrow Wilson, *Constitutional Government in the United States* (New York: Columbia University Press, 1908).

2. David B. Truman, *The Governmental Process* (New York: Alfred A. Knopf, 1951), p. 52.

3. Among the many works to take this approach, see V.O. Key, *Public Opinion and American Democracy* (New York: Alfred A. Knopf, 1965).

4. Among the first to write in this manner was David Easton, *The Political System* (New York: Alfred A. Knopf, 1953).

5. Lawrence Friedman, *American Law* (New York: W.W. Norton, 1984), p. 32.

6. Calvin MacKenzie, *American Government: Politics and Policy* (New York: Random House, 1986), p. 4.

7. Thomas Dye, *Understanding Public Policy*, 6th ed. (Englewood Cliffs, NJ: Prentice-Hall, 1987), p. 2.

8. B. Guy Peters, *American Public Policy: Promise and Performance*, 3d ed. (Chatham, NJ: Chatham House, 1993), p. 2.

9. David Robertson and Dennis Judd, *The Development of American Public Policy: The Structure of Policy Restraint* (Glenview, IL: Scott, Foresman, 1989), p. 7.

10. Easton, op. cit., *The Political System*, p. 129.

11. "Clear Benefits of Clean Air Act Come at a Cost," *The Wall Street Journal*, November 11, 1993, pp. B1, B5.

12. Noted historian Arthur M. Schlesinger, Jr., makes this point in *The Imperial Presidency* (Boston: Houghton Mifflin, 1973), pp. 178–87.

13. See "Clinton's Signature Launches Historic Overhaul of Welfare," *Los Angeles Times*, August 23, 1996, pp. A1, A26, A27.

14. *Texas v. Johnson*, 491. U.S. 397.

15. For a brief history of the regulatory movement, see Larry N. Gerston, Cynthia Fraleigh, and Robert Schwab, *The Deregulated Society* (Pacific Grove, CA: Brooks/Cole, 1988), pp. 7–17.

16. Two different approaches to this discussion are: Milton Friedman and Rose Friedman, *Free To Choose* (New York: Harcourt, Brace, Jovanovich, 1979); and Michael Reagan, *Regulation* (Boston: Little, Brown: 1987).

17. Michael Reagan and John Sanzone, *The New Federalism*, 2d ed. (New York: Oxford University Press, 1981), p. 158.

18. Virgina Gray, Herbert Jacob, and Robert B. Albritton, *Politics in the American States*, 5th ed. (Glenview, IL: Scott, Foresman/Little, Brown, 1990), p. 74.

19. For a summary of these tools of citizen government, see Ann O'M. Bowman and Richard C. Kearney, *State and Local Government* (Boston: Houghton Mifflin, 1990), pp. 119–26.

20. Dennis S. Ippolito, *The Budget and National Politics* (San Francisco: Freeman, 1978), p. 27.

21. Thomas R. Dye and Harmon Zeigler, *The Irony of Democracy*, 9th ed. (Belmont, CA: Wadsworth, 1993), p. 276.

22. See "Military Prepares Deeper Cutbacks," *San Jose Mercury News*, November 24, 1991, pp. 1A, 24A; and "As Political Heat Is Turned Up in Cold War Foe, Some in U.S. Try to Chill Ferver for Defense Cuts," *The Wall Street Journal*, March 23, 1993, p. A16.

23. "Entitlements Seen Taking Up Nearly All Taxes by 2012," *Los Angeles Times*, August 9, 1994, pp. A1, A23.

24. See Lester Thurow, *The Zero-Sum Society* (New York: Penguin, 1981), pp. 9–11.

25. David Osborne and Ted Gaebler, *Reinventing Government* (New York: Penguin, 1992).

26. For two classic treatments on the impact of technological change, see Emile Durkheim, *The Division of Labor in Society*, 1933 (New York: Free Press, 1964); and Ferdinand Tonnies, *Fundamental Concepts of Sociology* (New York: American, 1940).

27. Gabriel Almond and G. Bingham Powell, *Comparative Politics* (Boston: Little, Brown, 1966), p. 95.

28. Rudi Volti, *Society and Technological Change*, 3d ed. (New York: St. Martin's Press, 1995).

29. Theodore Lowi, *The End of Liberalism*, 2d ed. (New York: W.W. Norton, 1979), p. 23.

Notes to Chapter 2

1. Robert Eyestone, *From Issues to Public Policy* (New York: John Wiley and Sons, 1978), p. 78.

2. John W. Kingdon, *Agendas, Alternatives, and Public Policies* (Boston: Little, Brown, 1994), pp. 177–78.

3. For example, see "Cost Could Be Key to Health Care Reform," *Los Angeles Times*, October 3, 1993, pp. A1, A10; and "Americans Still Support Reform for Health Care, But Poll Finds Zeal Waning and Fear of Change," *The Wall Street Journal*, June 16, 1994, p. A20.

4. Thomas R. Dye, *Understanding Public Policy*, 6th ed. (Englewood Cliffs, NJ: Prentice-Hall, 1987), p. 325.

5. For a detailed discussion of the event and its aftermath, see Walter A. Rosenbaum, *Environmental Politics and Policy*, 3d ed. (Washington, DC: CQ Press, 1995), pp. 130–31.

6. See "What if a Cure Is Far Off," *Newsweek*, June 21, 1993, p. 70.

7. Sidney Verba and Norman H. Nie, *Participation in America* (New York: Harper and Row, 1972), p. 105.

8. Clyde Wilcox, *The Latest American Revolution?* (New York: St. Martin's Press, 1995), p. 24.

9. Steven J. Rosenstone and John Mark Hansen, *Mobilization, Participation, and Democracy in America* (New York: Macmillan, 1993), p. 143.

10. Robert L. Lineberry, *American Public Policy* (New York: Harper and Row, 1977), p. 63.

11. See John Martilla, "American Public Opinion: Evolving Questions of National Security," in Edward K. Hamilton, ed., *America's Global Interests* (New York: W.W. Norton, 1989), pp. 268–69.

12. For example, at the end of the Persian Gulf conflict in July 1991, results from a nationwide public opinion poll showed that Americans favored U.S. participation by a margin of 78 percent to 17 percent. Within a few months, another nationwide survey indicated that only 12 percent of those interviewed considered national security and foreign policy as the country's most important problem, compared with 41 percent who cited domestic issues and 35 percent who listed the economy. See "Holiday Pride Tempered by Ongoing Concern About Hussein," *Los Angeles Times*, July 4, 1991, p. A5; and "Voters Voice Dismay about Nation's Course a Year before Election," *The Wall Street Journal*, November 1, 1991, pp. A1, A16.

13. "State Economy in Recovery, UCLA Finds," *Los Angeles Times*, March 30, 1994, pp. A1, A28.

14. For a discussion on the causes of deficits and their consequences, see Denise E. Markovich and Ronald E. Pynn, *The American Political Economy* (Pacific Grove, CA: Brooks/Cole, 1988), pp. 148–65.

15. The issues leading up to and consequences of the collapse of the financial services sector are discussed in Larry N. Gerston, Cynthia Fraleigh, and Robert Schwab, *The Deregulated Society* (Belmont, CA: Wadsworth, 1988), pp. 122–36.

16. "Toting Up Blame for S&L Crisis," *Los Angeles Times*, September 16, 1990, pp. A1, A32, A33.

17. Lynton K. Caldwell, *Man and His Environment: Policy and Administration* (New York: Harper and Row, 1975), pp. 147–48.

18. James R. Beniger, "The Control Revolution," in Albert H. Teich, ed., *Technology and the Future*, 6th ed. (New York: St. Martin's Press, 1993), p. 43.

19. Caldwell, op. cit., p. 8.

20. Jacqueline Vaughn Switzer, *Environmental Politics* (New York: St. Martin's Press, 1994), pp. 257–60.

21. For a thorough review of how political attitudes and values are acquired, see Robert S. Erikson, Norman R. Luttbeg, and Kent L. Tedin, *American Public Opinion*, 4th ed. (New York: Macmillan, 1991), pp. 135–67. A comparative assessment is offered in Gabriel A. Almond and Sidney Verba, eds., *The Civic Culture Revisited* (Boston: Little, Brown, 1980).

22. Eyestone, op. cit., p. 70.

23. See Jo Freeman, *The Politics of Women's Liberation* (New York: David McKay, 1975), pp. 28–30.

24. For example, during the 1970s, Susan A. MacManus and Nikki R. Van Hightower found that male heads of households had per capita incomes almost twice as high as their female counterparts. See their "The Impacts of Local Government Tax Structures on Women: Inefficiencies and Ineqaulities," *The Social Science Journal*, vol. 14, no. 2 (April 1977), p. 103.

25. *New York State Club v. City of New York*, 108 S. Ct. 2225 (1988).

26. "Pay Gap Widens between Top Male, Female Executives," *San Jose Mercury News*, June 30, 1993, pp. 1A, 18A.

27. Hans J. Morganthau, *Politics Among Nations*, 3d ed. (New York: Alfred A. Knopf, 1960), p. 38.

28. "U.S. to Intercept Ships, Plans to Halt All of Iraq's Sea Trade," *Los Angeles Times*, August 13, 1990, pp. A1, A12.

29. "U.N. Gives Iraq until Jan. 15 to Leave Kuwait or Face War," *Los Angeles Times*, November 30, 1990, pp. A1, A18, A19.

30. "U.N. Issues Strict Terms as It Votes Formal End to Iraq War," *Los Angeles Times*, April 4, 1991, pp. A1, A6.

31. "The New, Dangerous Dominoes," *Los Angeles Times*, May 8, 1994, pp. A1, A14.

32. Phil Williams, "Foreign Policy," in Gillian Peele, Christopher J. Bailey, Bruce Cain, and B. Guy Peters, eds., *Developments in American Politics 2* (Chatham, NJ: Chatham House, 1995), pp. 292, 294.

33. Switzer, op. cit., p. 305.

34. "U.S. Unable to Formulate Competitiveness Strategy," *Los Angeles Times*, October 25, 1991, pp. A1, A18; and "How Japanese Foreign Aid Helps Japan's Economy," *San Jose Mercury News*, April 19, 1992, pp. 1A, 19A.

35. "Protectionism Is as American as Ice Cream," *San Jose Mercury News*, February 7, 1992.

36. See "Deals Pave the Way for Free-Trade Pact," *The Wall Street Journal*, December 2, 1994, p. A8.

37. Morganthau, op. cit., pp. 180–81.

38. See Charles W. Ostrom, Jr., "A Reactive Linkage Model of the U.S. Defense Expenditure Policymaking Process," *The American Political Science Review*, vol. 72, no. 3 (September 1978), p. 943.

39. Excerpts from "Defense Planning Guidance for the Fiscal Years 1994–1999," printed in *The New York Times*, March 8, 1992, pp. 1, 4.

40. See "Shifting Battle Lines in Arms Race," *Los Angeles Times*, August 8, 1993, pp. F1, 5.

41. "We're No.1 in the Arms Bazaar," *Los Angeles Times*, May 3, 1994, p. B7.

42. Henry Kissinger, *Nuclear Weapons and Foreign Policy* (New York: Doubleday Anchor, 1957), p. 177.

Notes to Chapter 3

1. Robert Eyestone, *From Social Issues to Public Policy* (New York: John Wiley and Sons, 1978), p. 71.

2. William Crotty, "The Role of the State in a Post–Cold War Society," in William Crotty, ed., *Post–Cold War Policy* (Chicago: Nelson-Hall, 1995), p. 53.

3. Samuel Kernell, *Going Public* (Washington, DC: CQ Press, 1986), pp. 83–97.

4. See "The Lost Chance," *Newsweek*, September 19, 1994, pp. 26–32.

5. During the 1996 presidential election campaign, Dole was quoted as saying "I'm Not Certain whether it's [Tobacco Is] addictive." *Los Angeles Times*, September 17, 1996, p. A16.

6. "Conservatives Tear a Page from Liberals' Book, 'Borking' Clinton's Nominees for Legal Positions," *The Wall Street Journal*, November 29, 1993, p. A16.

7. Henry R. Glick, *Courts, Politics and Justice*, 2d ed. (New York: McGraw-Hill, 1988), p. 5.

8. Guy Beneviste makes this point in *Regulation and Planning* (San Francisco: Boyd and Fraser, 1981), chapter 6.

9. See "FCC Angers Cable Firms, Aids Networks," *The Wall Street Journal*, April 2, 1993, pp. B1, B7; and "TV Stations across U.S. Wrestle with New Cable Rules," *Los Angeles Times*, April 30, 1993, pp. D1, D2.

10. For the classic definition and explanation of bureaucracy, see Max Weber, "Bureaucracy," in *From Max Weber: Essays in Sociology*, translated by H.H. Gerth and C. Wright Mills (New York: Oxford University Press, 1962), pp. 196–244.

11. George J. Gordon, *Public Administration in America*, 3d ed. (New York, St. Martin's Press, 1986), pp. 38–39.

12. Kenneth J. Meier, *Politics and the Bureaucracy*, 3d ed. (Pacific Grove, CA: Brooks/Cole, 1993), p. 117.

13. See "Dioxin Joins List of Costly False Alarms," *Los Angeles Times*, August 19, 1991, p. B5.

14. Roger W. Cobb and Charles D. Elder, *Participation in Politics: The Dynamics of Agenda-Building* (Baltimore: Johns Hopkins Press, 1972), p. 142.

15. E.E. Schattschneider, *The Semi-Sovereign People* (New York: Holt, Rinehart and Winston, 1960), pp. 7–8.

16. For an example of such an expose, see "Small Aircraft as Big Peril Flying in Deregulated Skies," *Los Angeles Times*, September 6, 1987, pp. P1, P2.

17. See "Mouse Wars Grow More Furious," *Los Angeles Times*, May 9, 1993, pp. A1, A14, A15.

18. Shanto Iyengar and Donald R. Kinder, *News that Matters* (Chicago: University of Chicago Press, 1987), p. 47.

19. Carol Greenwald, *Group Power* (New York: Praeger, 1977), p. 21.

20. Jeffrey M. Berry, *The Interest Group Society*, 2d ed. (Glenview, IL: Scott, Foresman, 1989), p. 211.

21. Theodore J. Lowi, *The End of Liberalism*, 2d ed. (New York: W.W. Norton, 1979), p. 51.

22. William P. Browne, "Organized Interests, Grassroots Confidants, and Congress," in Allan J. Cigler and Burdett Loomis, eds., *Interest Group Politics*, 4th ed. (Washington, DC: CQ Press, 1995), p. 295.

23. For a historical account of this long-term relationship, see Grant McConnell, *Private Power and American Democracy* (New York: Alfred A. Knopf, 1967), pp. 215–43.

24. "Stuck on the Honey Subsidy," *Los Angeles Times*, March 21, 1993, pp. A1, A26.

25. George C. Edwards, III and Ira Sharkansky, *The Policy Predicament* (San Francisco: W.H. Freeman, 1978), p. 226.

26. Gregory R. Weiher, "Post–Cold War Social Welfare Policy: Limited Options," in William Crotty, ed., *Post–Cold War Policy* (Chicago: Nelson-Hall, 1995), p. 350.

27. Hannah Fenichel Pitkin, *The Concept of Representation* (Berkeley: University of California Press, 1967), p. 97.

28. Quoted in "Clinton Denounces 'Militia' Extremists," *San Jose Mercury News*, May 6, 1995, p. 5A.

29. "Government Waste Rampant, GAO says," *Los Angeles Times*, January 8, 1993, p. A26.

30. See "Clinton Moves to Streamline Government," *The Wall Street Journal*, September 8, 1993, p. A2; and "Gore vs. Grace: Dueling Reinventions Show How Clinton, Reagan Views of Government Differ," *The Wall Street Journal*, September 6, 1993, p. A10.

31. "Most Americans Favor Reforms in Nation's Health Care System," *Los Angeles Times*, February 2, 1990, pp. A1, A26.

32. "Health-Care Battle," *The Wall Street Journal*," September 23, 1993, pp. A1, A6.

33. "GOP Unveils Its Overhaul of Medicare," *Los Angeles Times*, September 15, 1995, pp. A1, A16.

34. Gabriel Sheffer, "Reversibility of Policies and Patterns of Politics," *Policy Studies Journal*, vol. 5, 1977, p. 548.

35. Eyestone, op. cit., p. 118.

36. Roger Cobb, Jennie Keith-Ross, and Marc Howard Ross, "Agenda Building as a Comparative Political Process," *The American Political Science Review*, vol. LXX, no. 1 (March 1976), p. 127.

37. See, for example, Robert S. Erikson, Norman R. Luttbeg, and Kent L. Tedin, *American Public Opinion: Its Orgins, Content, and Impact*, 4th ed. (New York: Macmillan, 1991), chapters 4, 5; Bernard Hennessy, *Public Opinion*, 5th ed. (Pacific Grove, CA: Brooks/Cole, 1985), chapter 6; Harry Holloway with John George, *Public Opinion*, 2d ed. (New York: St. Martin's Press, 1986), chapter 14.

38. See Michael Parenti, *Land of Idols* (New York: St. Martin's Press, 1994), chapter 12.

39. "Extremism in America," *U.S. News and World Report*, May 8, 1995, pp. 27–44.

40. "The Plot," *Newsweek*, May 8, 1995, pp. 28–34.

41. For a collection of the myriad interpretations concerning Kennedy's death, see Bradley A. Greenberg and Edwin B. Parker, eds., *The Kennedy Assassination and the American Public* (Stanford: Stanford University Press, 1965).

42. This argument is made by John J. Harrigan, *Empty Dreams, Empty Pockets* (New York: Macmillan, 1993).

43. See, for example, Terence H. Qualter, "The Role of the Mass Media in Limiting the Public Agenda," in Michael Margolis and Gary A. Mauser, eds., *Manipulating Public Opinion* (Pacific Grove, CA: Brooks/Cole, 1989), pp. 151–53.

44. See "The Revolving Door," *Los Angeles Times*, March 13, 1994, pp. D1, D4, D6.

45. Clifton McCleskey, *Political Power and American Democracy* (Pacific Grove, CA: Brooks/Cole, 1989), p. 11.

46. E.E. Schattschneider, *The Semi-Sovereign People* (New York: Holt, Rinehart and Winston, 1960), p. 71.

47. For the classic treatment of decision-making theory as an open governmental process responsive to the issues of the day, see Robert A. Dahl, *Who Governs?* (New Haven, CT: Yale University Press, 1961).

48. Peter Bachrach and Morton S. Baratz, "Two Faces of Power," *The American Political Science Review*, vol. LXV, no. 4 (December 1971), p. 1088.

49. Sidney Verba and Norman H. Nie, *Participation in America* (New York: Harper and Row, 1972), p. 271.

50. Steven J. Rosenstone and John Mark Hansen, *Mobilization, Participation and Democracy in America* (New York: Macmillan, 1993), p, 80.

51. John W. Kingdon, *Agendas, Alternatives, and Public Policies* (Boston: Little, Brown, 1984), p. 210.

52. David B. Robertson and Dennis R. Judd, *The Development of American Public Policy* (Glenview, IL: Little, Brown, 1989), pp. 9–12.

53. Donald C. Baumer and Carl E. Van Horn, *The Politics of Unemployment* (Washington, DC: C.Q. Press, 1985), p. 38.

54. Norman J. Ornstein and Shirley Elder, *Interest Groups, Lobbying and Policymaking* (Washington, DC: CQ Press, 1971), p. 288.

55. For instance, see Dennis Pirages, *Managing Political Conflict* (New York: Praeger, 1976), p. 81.

56. Michael Parenti, *Democracy for the Few*, 5th ed. (New York: St. Martin's Press, 1988), p. 69.

Notes to Chapter 4

1. Charles O. Jones, *An Introduction to the Study of Public Policy*, 3d ed. (Pacific Grove, CA: Brooks/Cole, 1984), pp. 110–11.

2. The classic explanation of the iron triangle policy network is found in Theodore J. Lowi, *The End of Liberalism*, 2d ed. (New York: W.W. Norton, 1979).

3. Charles F. Bonser, Eugene B. McGregor, Jr., and Clinton V. Oster, Jr., *Policy Choices and Public Action* (Upper Saddle River, NJ: Prentice Hall, 1996), p. 25.

4. Robert L. Lineberry, *American Public Policy* (New York: Harper and Row, 1977), p. 43.

5. For an overview of the constitutional framework with respect to the management of political power, see David C. Nice and Patricia Fredericksen, *The Politics of Intergovernmental Relations,* 2d ed. (Chicago: Nelson-Hall, 1995).

6. David B. Robertson and Dennis R. Judd, *The Development of American Public Policy* (Glenview, IL: Scott, Foresman, 1989), p. 3.

7. Randall B. Ripley, *Congress: Process and Policy*, 4th ed. (New York: W.W. Norton, 1988), p. 40.

8. Edward V. Schneier and Bertram Gross, *Congress Today* (New York: St. Martin's Press, 1993), p. 4.

9. For a lengthy discussion and analysis of the post-1994 election changes in the House of Representatives, see C. Lawrence Evans and Walter J. Oleszek, *Congress under Fire: Reform Politics and the Republican Majority* (Boston: Houghton Mifflin, 1997), pp. 87–108.

10. Lowi, op. cit., pp. 274, 276.

11. This term is used by Charles O. Jones in "House Leadership in an Age of Reform," in Frank H. Mackaman, ed., *Understanding Congressional Leadership* (Washington, DC: Congressional Quarterly Press, 1992), p. 126.

12. Stephen D. Van Beek, *Post-Passage Politics* (Pittsburgh: University of Pittsburgh Press, 1995), p. 5.

13. "Spending Pact Marks Major Retreat by GOP Leaders," *The Wall Street Journal*, September 30, 1996, p. A18.

14. See "How a House Staffer Wields Great Power over Policy Decisions," *The Wall Street Journal*, June 30, 1989, pp. A1, A9.

15. For a case study on the impact of staff, see Janet M. Martin, *Lessons from the Hill* (New York: St. Martin's Press, 1994), pp. 69–73.

16. The ability of Newt Gingrich to instill discipline in the ranks of the Republican majority during the 104th Congress stands as an exception to the democratization phenomenon and, indeed, may well account for much of the GOP's success during this period. See "GOP's Rare Year Owes Much to How Gingrich Disciplined the House," *The Wall Street Journal*, December 18, 1995, pp. A1, A8.

17. Dan Rostenkowski, chair of the House Ways and Means Committee, was defeated for reelection in 1994 after coming under attack for numerous campaign violations and mismanagement of government funds. Bob Packwood, chair of the Senate Finance Committee, began a long, painful slide in 1995 after a Senate Ethics Committee determined at least eighteen possible instances of sexual harassment as well as obstruction of efforts to investigate the matter. House Speaker Newt Gingrich was fined three hundred thousand dollars by the House for ethics violations in 1997.

18. David J. Vogler, *The Politics of Congress*, 6th ed. (Madison, WI: Brown and Benchmark, 1993), p. 263.

19. George C. Edwards III and Stephen J. Wayne, *Presidential Leadership*, 3d ed. (New York: St. Martin's Press, 1994), pp. 6–7.

20. James W. Davis, *The American Presidency* (New York: Harper and Row, 1987), p. 12.

21. Edwards and Wayne, op. cit., p. 386.

22. See "U.S. Efforts to Bail Out Mexico Are Still Hanging in the Balance," *New York Times*, April 2, 1995, pp. 1, 8.

23. Arthur M. Schlesinger, Jr., is one of the many who make this argument. See his *The Imperial Presidency* (Boston: Houghton Mifflin, 1973).

24. Samuel Kernell, *Going Public* (Washington, DC: CQ Press, 1986), p. 204.

25. For an assessment of the management of domestic issues by the Clinton presidency, see Barbara Sinclair, "Trying to Govern Positively in a Negative Era: Clinton and the 103rd Congress," in Colin Campbell and Bert A. Rockman, eds., *The Clinton Presidency: First Appraisals* (Chatham, NJ: Chatham House, 1995), pp. 88–123.

26. David Stoesz, *Small Change: Domestic Policy under the Clinton Administration* (White Plains, NY: Longman, 1996), p. 217.

27. Mary M. Walker, *The Evolution of the United States Supreme Court* (Morristown, NJ: General Learning Press, 1974), p. 3.

28. So fundamental was this change that Michael D. Reagan and John G. Sanzone refer to it as the "Constitutional Revolution of 1937." See their book, *The New Federalism*, 2d ed. (New York: Oxford University Press, 1981).

29. Stephen L. Wasby, *The Supreme Court in the Federal Judicial System* (Chicago: Nelson-Hall, 1988), p. 296.

30. See "The Limits of Commerce," *Newsweek*, May 8, 1995, p. 72.

31. *U.S. Term Limits v. Thornton*, 93–1456. Quoted from "High Court Bars States from Limiting Congressional Terms," *Los Angeles Times*, May 23, 1995, pp. A1, A14.

32. Robert A. Dahl, *Pluralist Democracy in the United States* (Chicago: Rand McNally, 1967), p. 170.

33. Nathan Glazer, *Affirmative Discrimination* (New York: Basic Books, 1978), p. 208.

34. Henry J. Abraham, *The Judiciary*, 9th ed. (Madison, WI: Brown and Benchmark, 1987), p. 81.

35. Peter Woll, *Constitutional Democracy*, 2d ed. (Boston: Little, Brown, 1986), p. 287.

36. See Donald M. Snow and Eugene Brown, *Puzzle Palaces and Foggy Bottom* (New York: St. Martin's Press, 1994), pp. 174–75.

37. See "FDA Issues Rules for Backing Up Vitamin Claims," *Los Angeles Times*, December 30, 1993, pp. A1, A16.

38. Carl Friedrich initially wrote this assessment in 1936, and was reprinted in 1978 as part of a collection of essays. See Carl J. Friedrich, "Public Policy and the Nature of Administrative Responsibility," in Francis E. Rourke, ed., *Bureaucratic Power in National Politics*, 3d ed. (Boston: Little, Brown, 1978), p. 401.

39. Herbert A. Simon, Donald W. Smithburg, and Victor A. Thompson, "The Struggle for Organizational Survival," in Francis E. Rourke, ed., *Bureaucratic Power in National Politics,* 3d ed. (Boston: Little Brown, 1978), p. 28.

40. Milton and Rose Friedman, *Free to Choose* (New York: Avon, 1981), p. 284.

41. Randall B. Ripley and Grace A. Franklin, *Congress, the Bureaucracy and Public Policy*, 4th ed. (Chicago: Dorsey, 1987), pp. 86, 88.

42. Jeffrey M. Stonecash, *American State and Local Politics* (Orlando, FL: Harcourt Brace, 1995), p. 410.

43. See Ann O'M. Bowman and Richard C. Kearney, *State and Local Government* (Boston: Houghton Mifflin, 1990), pp. 121–26.

44. See Larry N. Gerston and Terry Christensen, *California Politics and Government*, 3d ed. (Belmont, CA: Wadsworth, 1995), pp. 18–19.

45. E.E. Schattschneider, *The Semi-Sovereign People* (New York: Holt, Rinehart and Winston, 1960), p. 138.

Notes to Chapter 5

1. *Cherokee Nation v. Georgia*, 5 Peters 1 (1831): 302.

2. *Worchester v. Georgia*, 6 Peters 515 (1832): 302, 338.

3. Alfred H. Kelley and Winifred A. Harbison, *The American Constitution* (New York: W.W. Norton, 1948), p. 303.

4. Michael T. Hayes, *Incrementalism and Public Policy* (White Plains, NY: Longman, 1992), p. 2.

5. David Truman's work, *The Governmental Process*, epitomizes the rich body of literature that dominated American political thought for more than half of the twentieth century. Writing in 1951, Truman explained policy as the synthesis of interaction between interest groups and government institutions. When the second edition was published twenty years later, Truman defended the contemporary utility of his approach: "The interest-group focus of *The Governmental Process* has, in the intervening years, become a major emphasis—perhaps a predominant one—in political science. . . . What was in 1950 a somewhat unusual way of looking at the governmental scene has become a part of the conventional wisdom of the discipline." See David Truman, *The Governmental Process*, 2d ed. (New York: Alfred A. Knopf, 1971), p. xx.

6. Paul Berman, "The Study of Macro- and Micro-Implementation," *Public Policy*, vol. 26, no. 2 (Spring 1978), p. 158.

7. Randall B. Ripley and Grace A. Franklin, *Congress, the Bureaucracy, and Public Policy*, 5th ed. (Pacific Grove, CA: Brooks/Cole, 1991), pp. 13–14.

8. For an excellent discussion of this matrix, see Kenneth J. Meier, *Politics and the Bureaucracy*, 3d ed. (Pacific Grove, CA: Brooks/Cole, 1993), chapter 4.

9. James P. Lester and Joseph Stewart, Jr., *Public Policy: An Evolutionary Approach* (Minneapolis/St. Paul: West, 1996), pp. 98–99.

10. Charles E. Lindblom, *The Policy-Making Process*, 2d ed. (Englewood Cliffs, NJ: Prentice Hall, 1980), p. 64.

11. George J. Gordon, *Public Administration in America*, 3d ed. (New York: St. Martin's Press, 1986), p. 122.

12. Several implementation scholars draw similar conclusions. Among them are: Malcolm L. Goggin, Ann O'M. Bowman, James P. Lester, and Laurence J. O'Toole, Jr., *Implementation Theory and Practice* (New York: Harper/Collins, 1990), p. 173; Charles O. Jones, *An Introduction to the Study of Public Policy*, 3d ed. (Monterey, CA: Brooks/Cole, 1984), p. 166; Robert L. Lineberry, *American Public Policy* (New York: Harper and Row, 1977), pp. 70–71; and Randall B. Ripley and Grace A. Franklin, *Policy Implementation and Bureaucracy*, 2d ed. (Chicago: Dorsey, 1986), pp. 10–11.

13. Meier, op. cit., p. 2.

14. Steven Thomas Seitz, *Bureaucracy, Policy and the Public* (St. Louis: C.V. Mosby, 1968), p. 164.

15. Quoted in "FDA Goes up against a Newly Revived GOP," *Los Angeles Times*, January 2, 1995, pp. A1, A20.

16. See Paul Light, *Artful Work* (New York: Random House, 1985), pp. 37, 106.

17. "Medicare Well Could Run Dry by '98, Trustees Say," *Los Angeles Times*, April 7, 1993, p. A16.

18. Although his framework is discussed in several books and articles, Lowi's discussion first appeared in a 1964 article. See Theodore J. Lowi, "American Business, Public Policy, Case-Studies and Political Theory," *World Politics* 16 (July 1964), pp. 677–715. Several scholars have embellished upon Lowi's ap-

proach, the most prominent of whom, Paul Salisbury, folds in a fourth category, self-regulation, as a component of two themes, allocative policies and structural policies. See Paul H. Salisbury, "The Analysis of Public Policy: A Search for Theories and Roles," in Austin Ranney, ed., *Political Science and Public Policy* (Chicago: Markham, 1968), pp. 151–75. In yet another variation of a theme, Ripley and Franklin carve out a fourfold approach that includes distributive policy, competitive regulatory policy, protective regulatory policy, and redistributive policy; see Ripley and Franklin, op. cit., pp. 71–91.

19. Theodore J. Lowi, *The End of Liberalism*, 2d ed. (New York: W.W. Norton, 1979), p. 274.

20. With respect to the Federal Communications Commission, see Erwin G. Krasnow, Lawrence D. Longley, and Herbert A. Terry, *The Politics of Broadcast Regulation*, 3d ed. (New York: St. Martin's Press, 1982), pp. 37–42.

21. See "Deficit-Cutting Bill Bears a Resemblance to 1990 Predecessor," *The Wall Street Journal*, August 8, 1993, pp. A3, A9; and "Clinton's Welfare Proposal Falls Short," *San Jose Mercury News*, June 12, 1994, pp. A1, A10.

22. Meier, op. cit., p. 109.

23. Jacqueline Vaughn Switzer, *Environmental Politics* (New York: St. Martin's Press, 1994), p. 56.

24. See "EPA Declares 'Passive' Smoke a Human Carcinogen," *The Wall Street Journal*, January 6, 1993, pp. B1, and B5; and "EPA Report Sparks Antismoking Plans," *The Wall Street Journal*, January 7, 1993, pp. B1, B6.

25. Meier, op. cit., p. 100.

26. For a comprehensive discussion relating to the models of federalism, see David C. Nice, *Federalism: The Politics of Intergovernmental Relations* (New York: St. Martin's Press, 1987), pp. 4–13.

27. *Brown v. Board of Education of Topeka*, 347 U.S. 483.

28. "Integration Questions Linger Four Decades Later," *Los Angeles Times*, May 15, 1994, pp. A1, A12.

29. The new law limits eligibility for food stamps to three months per three-year period among able-bodied adults, ages eighteen to fifty, without children and without at least half-time jobs. Source: "Food Stamp Cuts to Take Toll on Unemployed," *Los Angeles Times*, October 5, 1996, pp. A1, A18.

30. "After GATT," *Los Angeles Times*, November 29, 1994, p. A5.

31. David R. Beam and Timothy J. Conlon, "The Growth of Intergovernmental Mandates in an Era of Deregulation and Decentralization," in Lawrence J. O'Toole, Jr., *American Intergovernmental Relations*, 2d ed. (Washington, DC: CQ Press, 1993), p. 323.

32. See David B. Walker, *Toward a Functioning Federalism* (Cambridge, MA: Winthrop Publishers, 1981), p. 10. Walker refers to the increase in federal demands as "creeping conditionalism."

33. Robert L. Lineberry, *American Public Policy* (New York: Harper and Row, 1977), p. 78.

34. Jones, op. cit., p. 179.

35. Marc K. Landy, Marc J. Roberts, and Stephen R. Thomas, *The Environmental Protection Agency*, expanded ed. (New York: Oxford University Press, 1994), p. 314.

36. See "Not in My Garage: Clean Air Act Triggers Backlash as Its Focus

Shifts to Driving Habits," *The Wall Street Journal*, January 25, 1995, pp. A1, A11.

37. Lineberry, op. cit., pp. 84–85.

38. Lowi makes this argument persuasively in *The End of Liberalism*, op. cit., pp. 279–94.

39. Lowi, *The End of Liberalism*, op. cit., p. 106.

40. "Administration Outlines Policies to Help Small Firms," *The Wall Street Journal*, June 15, 1995, p. B2.

41. Gary C. Bryner, *Bureaucratic Discretion* (New York: Pergamon, 1987), p. 87.

42. "The Superfund Cleanup: Mired in Its Own Mess," *Los Angeles Times*, May 10, 1993, pp. A1, A10.

43. For a discussion of the deterioration of Clinton's National Community Service Program, see Richard E. Cohen, *Changing Course in Washington: Clinton and the New Congress* (New York: Macmillan, 1994), pp. 200–201.

44. "Clinton Unveils GOP-Style Plan for State Block Grants," *Los Angeles Times*, February 1, 1995, pp. A1, A15.

45. "Different Drum: GOP, Despite Slips, Manages to Change Government's Course," *The Wall Street Journal*, April 7, 1995, pp. A1, A4.

46. See Walter A. Rosenbaum, *Environmental Politics and Policy*, 3d ed. (Washington, DC: CQ Press, 1995), pp. 269–77.

47. See "Nuclear Utilities Face Immense Expenses in Dismantling Plants," *The Wall Street Journal*, January 25, 1993, pp. A1, A7.

48. Lawrence C. Dodd and Richard L. Schott, *Congress and the Administrative State* (New York: John Wiley and Sons, 1979), p. 173.

49. *Immigration and Naturalization Service v. Chadha*, 448 U.S. 607 (1983).

50. "Clinton Casts His First Veto," *San Jose Mercury News*, June 8, 1995, p. 10A.

51. Many Republicans as well as Democrats agreed that the 1995 spending fights were at least as philosophical in nature as they were programmatic in design. In the words of new House Appropriations Committee Chair Bob Livingston, "[Vice President] Al Gore wanted to reinvent government, we want to reduce it." See "House Republicans Elect New Leaders, Plan Bill in Early '95 to Cut Spending," *The Wall Street Journal*, December 6, 1994, p. A22.

52. Kenneth J. Meier, *Politics and the Bureaucracy* (North Scituate, MA: Duxbury, 1979), p. 52.

Notes to Chapter 6

1. Lawrence B. Mohr, *Impact Analysis for Program Evaluation* (Pacific Grove, CA: Brooks/Cole, 1988), pp. 2–3.

2. Several studies during the 1960s and 1970s attempted to measure the outcomes of public policies and programs without regard to whether they were "good" or "bad." For an early, well-respected effort, see James Coleman, *Equality of Educational Opportunity* (Washington, DC: U.S. Government Printing Office, 1966).

3. Dennis Palumbo and Steven Maynard-Moody, *Contemporary Public Administration* (New York: Longman, 1991), pp. 284–85.

4. Frank Fischer, *Evaluating Public Policy* (Chicago: Nelson-Hall, 1995), p. 19.

5. Robert Blank and Janna C. Merrick, *Human Reproduction, Emerging Technologies, and Conflicting Rights* (Washington, DC: CQ Press, 1995), p. 215.

6. See James P. Lester and Joseph Stewart, Jr., *Public Policy: An Evolutionary Approach* (St. Paul: West, 1996), p. 121.

7. The strength of internal evaluative efforts, it would seem, depends on a variety of factors, including the issue, the mood of Congress, and the agency's input. One example of the CBO's adhering to its objective is cited with regard to a recent education bill. See Janet M. Martin, *Lessons from the Hill* (New York: St. Martin's Press, 1994), p. 105.

8. Lester and Stewart, op. cit., pp. 121–22.

9. "How Cigarette Makers Keep Health Question 'Open' Year after Year," *The Wall Street Journal*, February 11, 1993, pp. A1, A6.

10. Peter H. Rossi and Howard E. Freeman, *Evaluation: A Systematic Approach*, 5th ed. (Newbury Park, CA: Sage, 1993), p. 164.

11. For a discussion of this chapter of economic history, see Larry N. Gerston, Cynthia Fraleigh, and Robert Schwab, *The Deregulated Society* (Pacific Grove, CA: Brooks/Cole, 1988), pp. 128–139.

12. Rudi Volti, *Society and Technological Change*, 3d ed. (New York: St. Martin's Press, 1995), pp. 118–21.

13. See Walter A. Rosenbaum, *Environmental Politics and Policy*, 3d ed. (Washington, DC: CQ Press, 1995), p. 219.

14. Quoted in "Endangered Species Act Is Now Looking to Save Itself," *Los Angeles Times*, June 6, 1995, p. A13.

15. "Minimal Impact from Minimum Wage," *The Wall Street Journal*, April 19, 1996, p. A2.

16. For a discussion of exploratory research issues, see Peter J. Haas and J. Fred Springer, *Policy Research and Public Decisions: Concepts and Cases for Public Administration* (New York: Garland, 1997), pp. 25–26.

17. For a discussion of approaches to experimental design, see Thomas M. Meenaghan and Keith M. Kilty, *Policy Analysis and Research Technology* (Chicago: Lyceum, 1994), pp. 195–200.

18. For a history of the issues concerning tobacco and government regulation, see A. Lee Fritschler and James M. Hoefler, *Smoking and Politics*, 5th ed. (Englewood Cliffs, NJ: Prentice Hall, 1996).

19. See "Direct Link Found between Smoking and Lung Cancer," *The New York Times*, October 18, 1996, pp. A1, A16.

20. Emil J. Posavac and Raymond G. Carey discuss the value of metaevaluation in *Program Evaluation: Methods and Case Studies*, 3d ed. (Englewood Cliffs, NJ: Prentice-Hall, 1989), pp. 281–85.

21. See "1992 Cost of Immigrants $18 Billion, Report Says," *Los Angeles Times*, November 5, 1993, pp. A1, A31.

22. See "Immigrants a Boon to State, Study Says," *Los Angeles Times,* June 10, 1996, pp. A3, A14.

23. For an excellent assessment of the inconsistencies surrounding immigration data, see "Data Sheds Heat, Not Light, on Immigration," *Los Angeles Times*, November 21, 1993, pp. A1, A24.

24. David Easton, "An Approach to the Analysis of Political Systems," *World Politics* 9, no. 3 (April 1957), pp. 383–400.

25. Fischer, op. cit., p. 224.

26. Ronald D. Sylvia, Kathleen M. Sylvia, and Elizabeth M. Gunn, *Program Planning and Evaluation for the Public Manager*, 2d ed. (Prospect Heights, IL: Waveland Press, 1997).

Notes to Chapter 7

1. Rudi Volti, *Society and Technological Change*, 3d ed. (New York: St. Martin's Press, 1995), pp. 119–21.

2. For a discussion of the precarious condition of the nation's drinking water supply, see Walter A. Rosenbaum, *Environmental Politics and Policy* (Washington, DC: CQ Press, 1995), pp. 227–29.

3. An excellent summary of the history of term limits debate was written by Fred R. Harris, *In Defense of Congress* (New York: St. Martins Press, 1995), pp. 48–52. A contemporary debate of term limits question is found in an exchange of essays in Robert E. DiClerico and Allan S. Hammock, eds., *Points of View*, 6th ed. (New York: McGraw-Hill, 1995); see George F. Will, "Congress, Term Limits and the Recovery of Deliberative Democracy," pp. 176–80; and Norman Ornstein, "Term Limits Would Just Make Things Worse," pp. 181–83.

4. Quoted in *U.S. Term Limits v. Thornton*, 93–1456.

5. See Alan I. Abramowitz, "The United States: Political Culture under Stress," in Gabriel A. Almond and Sidney Verba, eds., *The Civic Culture Revisited* (Boston: Little, Brown, 1980), pp. 177–211.

6. Benjamin Page and Robert Shapiro, "The Rationality of Public Opinion," in Bruce Miroff, Raymond Seidelman, and Todd Swanstrom, eds., *Debating Democracy* (Boston: Houghton Mifflin, 1997), pp. 125–37.

7. Edward V. Schneier and Bertram Gross, *Legislative Strategy* (New York: St. Martin's Press, 1993), p. 120.

8. For a comprehensive discussion of the question of leadership, see James MacGregor Burns, *Leadership* (New York: Harper and Row Publishers, 1978).

9. Thomas R. Dye, *Power and Society*, 7th ed. (Belmont, CA: Wadsworth Publishing Company, 1996), p. 45.

INDEX

Larry N. Gerston is professor of political science at San Jose State University. In addition to *Public Policy Making: Process and Principles*, he is the author or co-author of five books on state and national policy making. Since 1980, Gerston has been the political analyst at KNTV in San Jose. He is also the principal of an independent survey research firm.